HE
SAID
WHAT?!

Other New Hope® books by Brenda Poinsett

Not My Will: Finding Peace with Things You Can't Change

Holiday Living: Using Year-Round Holidays to Build Faith and Family

*Unwrapping Martha's Joy: Having a Mary Christmas in
Your Heart and Home*

The Friendship Factor: Why Women Need Other Women

*Can Martha Have a Mary Christmas: Untangling Expectations
and Truly Experiencing Jesus*

Wonder Women of the Bible: Heroes of Yesterday Who Inspire Us Today

HE
SAID
WHAT?!

JESUS' AMAZING WORDS TO WOMEN

NEW HOPE®
PUBLISHERS
Gospel-Centered. Missions-Driven.

BIRMINGHAM, ALABAMA

New Hope® Publishers
PO Box 12065
Birmingham, AL 35202-2065
NewHopeDigital.com
New Hope Publishers is a division of WMU®.

Library of Congress Cataloging-in-Publication Data

Poinsett, Brenda.
 He said what?! : Jesus' amazing words to women / Brenda Poinsett.
    pages cm
  ISBN 978-1-59669-427-9 (sc)
  1. Jesus Christ--Relations with women. 2. Women in the Bible. 3. Jesus Christ--Words. I.
Title.
  BT590.W6P65 2015
  232.9'54--dc23
                              2014038092

Unless otherwise indicated, all Scripture quotations in this publication are from the Good News
Translation—Second Edition Copyright © 1992 by American Bible Society. Used by Permission.
     Scripture quotations taken from the 21st Century King James Version®, copyright © 1994.
Used by permission of Deuel Enterprises, Inc., Gary, SD 57237. All rights reserved.
     Scripture quotations marked KJV are taken from The Holy Bible, King James Version.
     Scripture quotations marked *The Message* are taken from *The Message* by Eugene H.
Peterson. Copyright © 1993, 1994, 1995, 1996, 2000, 2001, 2002. Used by permission of
NavPress Publishing Group.
     Scripture quotations marked NASB are taken from the New American Standard
Bible®, Copyright © 1960, 1962, 1963, 1968, 1971, 1972, 1973, 1975, 1977, 1995 by The Lockman
Foundation. Used by permission.
     Scripture quotations marked NIV are taken from the HOLY BIBLE, NEW
INTERNATIONAL VERSION®. NIV®. Copyright©1973, 1978, 1984, 2011 by Biblica, Inc.®
Used by permission. All rights reserved worldwide.
     Scripture quotations marked NKJV are taken from the New King James Version.
Copyright © 1982 by Thomas Nelson, Inc. Used by permission. All rights reserved.
     Scripture quotations marked RSV are taken from the Revised Standard Version of the
Bible, copyright 1952 [2nd edition, 1971] by the Division of Christian Education of the National
Council of the Churches of Christ in the U.S.A. Used by permission. All rights reserved.
     Scripture quotations marked Williams are taken from the *Williams New Testament, The New
Testament in the Language of the People*, by Charles B. Williams. Copyright © 1937, 1966, 1986 by
Holman Bible Publishers. Used by permission.
     Scripture quotations marked TLB are taken from *The Living Bible*, copyright© 1971. Used
by permission of Tyndale House Publishers, Inc., Wheaton, IL. All rights reserved.

ISBN-13: 978-1-59669-427-9

N154106 • 0315 • 2M1

To

Mary Rose

who lets

Jesus speak to her

Table of Contents

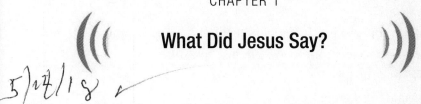

What Did Jesus Say?

5/24/18

WHEN OUR MIDDLE SON, JOEL, WAS IN COLLEGE, HE CALLED ONE SPRING day and said, "I won't be coming home for the summer. I've got a job."

"Oh, what are you going to be doing?"

"I'm going to be working for a moving company. I'm going to be driving a truck, a big wheeler." And then he said something that surprised me. He said, "I've always wanted to be a truck driver."

I wasn't surprised by his summer plans. What startled me was the word *always*. If he had said, "I dreamed about driving a big rig when I was a kid," I would have said, "Yes, I remember." He and his brothers played often with trucks in their sand pile, but Joel had gone on to other things such as sports and music. These activities dominated his attention. Joel played baseball and soccer, was in the high school band, participated in a drum and bugle corps, and was currently studying music performance and music engineering technology. And now he was saying that he *always* wanted to be a truck driver. As I hung up the phone, I thought to myself, *There's more to Joel than I know, even though he lived with us for almost 20 years.*

My friend Judy was a *homemaker* in every sense of the word. She managed her household well. She cooked; cleaned; kept a cozy, comfortable house; gardened; tended fruit trees; canned fruit and vegetables; cared for animals; entertained often; and played with her children. She did this graciously and never complained as some of her friends (ahem!) were prone to do. When our little prayer group met at her house, we always returned home inspired to do better. I personally felt if I ever "got it right" as a homemaker, I would be like Judy.

Imagine our surprise when at one of our gatherings she smiled broadly and said, "I need your prayers. I have a job interview."

"A what?"

"Yes, I found a job I would really like to have. I applied, and now I have an interview tomorrow. I'm just so excited."

"What's the job?"

"Managing a greenhouse."

We gulped and bowed our heads, but honestly it was hard to pray. Rather our thoughts were centered on the question, *Where was the domestic Judy we had always known?* We had no clue she wanted a job, let alone a demanding one like being a manager.

A co-worker and I attended a large meeting where right away we were aware that we stood out! In other words, our physical appearance significantly contrasted with the majority of those in attendance. I never thought anything about this, but Clarissa must have because on the way home, she kept referring to the attendees as "those people." She referred to the music of "those people," and she talked about the food "those people" had prepared and served. In those two words, my radar went up. Did Clarissa draw distinctive lines between "kinds" of people? After I got home and thought about this, I wondered if there wasn't some prejudice deep within her. Was she revealing a side of her that I had not seen before? And this led me to ask, *Were there other sides?*

The answer to this last question is yes, definitely. All of us are multifaceted beings with some of us being more complex than others. Sometimes long conversations are needed to draw out another person and to learn more about him or her, but as these incidents show, a few words can also be revealing. Just a few words can help us see a side of him or her that we didn't know existed. They open up new insights into who they are, what they might think, what they value, and what motivates them. We end up knowing them better.

This is true with friends, co-workers, and family members, and it's also true with Jesus. Take His conversations with women. Jesus spoke to women in short sentences and simple phrases. In a few words, He revealed various aspects of His nature (who He is, what He is like, what He desires, how He feels, what He values, etc.).

When I made it a point to study those conversations, I found myself being surprised in the same way I was surprised by Joel, Judy, and Clarissa. There was more of Him to know when I stopped to really listen.

5/15/18 ✓   ## HOW I LISTENED

There's a perfunctory way of reading what Jesus said, whether silently to yourself or orally before a group, where the words don't penetrate. They are just words and nothing more. No stirring of the soul occurs; no personal connection is made. I've found that to really listen to Jesus, I need to immerse myself in the conversation. I have to get a grip on it as if I were there, a part of the conversation.

To do this, I read and reread the passage. I investigate what was happening at the time. Where did the conversation take place? What prompted the conversation? What was happening in Jesus' life? What was happening in the woman's life? What cultural elements were involved? What customs were being practiced? What words were new to me? What do they mean? What was the significance of the conversation? What change occurred as a result of the conversation?

When you become engrossed like this in a biblical passage, the Word of God becomes "alive and active" (Hebrews 4:12 NIV), or as William Barclay's translation in his New Testament commentary, says, "The word of God is instinct with life." It "penetrates" deeply, "even to dividing soul and spirit, joints and marrow" (NIV). As His words penetrated my being, surprises started coming.

The surprise was sometimes in the context. In exploring the passage, I discovered things I didn't know—things that added to my understanding of Jesus.

But surprises also occurred because I was studying from a twenty-first-century perspective. At times, I even found myself scratching my head at something Jesus said. *How's that again? You said what?* Times have changed. Customs have changed, and even words have changed.

At other times, the surprise was in what Jesus' words really meant or what kind of effect they had on the woman involved. I found Him remarkable. I marveled at His sensitivity.

And frequently, the surprise was in what He said to me. You see when we immerse ourselves like I was doing in God's Word, our spiritual ears perk up. Our senses become alert. When we chew on a biblical passage, think about it, research it, we enter into a discovery mode, a learning mode, a place of receptivity. We provide an environment rich for receiving spiritual messages. Jesus will speak to us in a way that we know the words are for us. His words weren't meant just for women long ago, but they were meant for women today. They were meant for you and me.

The message He has for us may be one of conviction; the Word of God "judges the thoughts and attitudes of the heart" (Hebrews 4:12 NIV).

It may be challenging, indicating growth ahead.

It may be encouraging or motivating.

The message might provide direction or support.

Whatever the message, you will feel as if you have hit the Refresh button of your soul. You will feel renewed, your walk more confident, and your purpose clearer.

While immersion into Jesus' conversations contains various surprises, this in and of itself shouldn't be a surprise because the Gospels show people were often amazed and astonished by what Jesus said.

THE SURPRISING JESUS

People who interacted with Jesus when He walked on earth used words like *astonishing* and *amazing* to describe Him.

- The people in the temple area were amazed at His intelligent answers when He was 12 years old (Luke 2:42, 47), and so were His parents (v. 48)!

- When Jesus ended His Sermon on the Mount, "the people were astonished at his doctrine" (Matthew 7:28 KJV).
- When Jesus taught at the synagogue in Capernaum, they, too, "were astonished at his doctrine" (Mark 1:22).
- The reaction was the same when He answered satisfactorily a thorny question about whose wife will the woman who had been married seven times be in the Resurrection (Matthew 22:33).
- After Jesus commented on how hard it would be for rich people to enter into the kingdom of God, the disciples "were astonished out of measure" (Mark 10:26).
- When His spoken words were accompanied by a miracle, the astonishment reached an even higher degree. After He spoke words to a dead girl—words that brought her back to life, the people "were astonished with a great astonishment" (Mark 5:42).
- After speaking words that healed a deaf man, the people "were beyond measure astonished" (Mark 7:37).
- The scribes and chief priests feared Jesus "because all the people were astonished at His teaching" (Mark 11:18 NKJV).

How long has it been since you were amazed at Jesus? When have you reacted with "Wow!" to something He said? When have you used the word *surprising* to describe Jesus? Could your relationship use some refreshment? Would you like to know Him better? I say "better" because with Jesus, there's always more to know.

If you want your sense of wonder kindled, if you want some fresh insights into Jesus' nature, if you want to learn something new about Him, then I invite you to "look and listen" to conversations Jesus had with women and expect surprises.

SPIRITUAL SURPRISES

Some surprises may come simply because you learn something you didn't know. *Aha!* Knowledge does have a bearing on feeling spiritually alive.

Perhaps the surprise is learning something new regarding who Jesus is or what His nature is like, something that will make you say, "I didn't know that!"

Other surprises may come because of our twenty-first-century expectations. We may be shocked at what He said. *How could Jesus say such a thing?*

It may be getting to know Him better. *So this is what He is like. I understand Him so much better now* or *I feel closer to Him.* Increasing knowledge keeps a relationship vibrant.

Or an old truth—something you already knew—may be strengthened in a way that gives you new insight. *So this is what it means.*

Something may occur to you that you hadn't thought about before. *I never ever realized this in all the time I've served Him.*

If a haze of discouragement has been hovering overhead, it may dissipate. *Ah, I can see so much better now. Now I have hope. Now I can make it.*

If your energy for serving is about to die, now it may be revived. *So this is what He had in mind. I should have known.*

It could be any of a number of things, but the surprise will undoubtedly perk you up, give you hope, and restore your sense of wonder. *You mean me? The God of the universe is speaking to me?*

When Jesus speaks to me, His words touch the heart of who I am; when He speaks to you, His words will touch your heart. His is not a cliché message; He speaks to who we are and to where we are in our lives. He'll converse with us, clear up some of the confusion in our lives, add to our knowledge, nurture our sense of wonder, help us see more clearly, raise our hope level, warm our souls, give us insight for living, and motivate us to serve. When you experience any one of these things, when you hear what He is saying to you, that's when you will exclaim as I've been exclaiming, "Guess what He said to me!"

5/18/18

PART I

HOW'S THAT AGAIN?

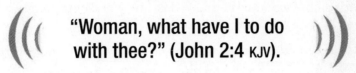

"Woman, what have I to do with thee?" (John 2:4 KJV).

5/18

WHEN ONE OF MY SONS WAS GOING THROUGH A ROUGH SPOT—THE kind that many young adults go through—I wanted to do something, but what? I was at a loss as to how to help. I decided to seek the counsel of another son. I said, "I would appreciate any advice you might have for me. How should I react? What should I do or say?"

He didn't immediately answer. As I sat waiting, I could see his mental wheels turning. I assumed he was thinking about possibilities, but I was to learn that he was deliberating about how honest he could be. After some time, he said, "You're really hard to talk to."

I said, "Well, sure, I could understand in cases like this."

He interrupted, "No, you don't understand. It is hard to tell you the good things too."

I couldn't believe what I was hearing. *It's hard to tell me good things?* His words were piercing, and I quickly excused myself so I could go cry! This was going to take some getting over.

I couldn't help but think of Mary, the mother of Jesus. Could she have been just as surprised when Jesus said to her, "Woman, what have I to do with thee?" (John 2:4 KJV). His question sounds harsh, especially considering it was uttered at a gala occasion.

5/19

WHEN JESUS SAID II

Mary and Jesus along with a few disciples were celebrating a marriage in Cana, a town near Mary's home in Nazareth. The ceremony was over, and the newlyweds were laughing, conversing, and eating with friends and family. (In Galilee, a newly married couple did not go away for a honeymoon; they stayed at home and entertained with an open house for several days.)

As this grand occasion progressed, something went wrong. The hosts ran out of wine! Failing to provide food and drink at any time would have been a problem. Hospitality in Palestine was a sacred duty, and it would be a terrible shame for the provisions to fail at a wedding. This was to be a time of joy! If the wine ran out, many guests would leave, and the celebration would abruptly end.

Perhaps the couple or their parents hadn't adequately planned ahead. Perhaps more people showed up than were expected. Whatever the cause, the "ruler of the feast," the one in charge, didn't notice what was happening. The bride and groom were blissfully unaware. Neither did the parents of the bride and groom. Mary, though, noticed.

MARY'S EAGLE EYES

Many women have an eye for picking up on what's happening around them, even when they are doing something else. Women's brains are constantly taking in and assimilating information from everything they see and hear.

For Mary, this capability had been in use for years, probably beginning when her children were small. She had learned to take in details of her surroundings while also watching her children. She had been hospitable many times, as most women in her culture were. She was experienced at hosting and helping with festive occasions for friends, relatives, and possibly the weddings of some of her other children.

This is why, at a wedding party, she could mingle and talk with guests, help with the food being served, and still notice that the wine had run out. And even though she wasn't in charge, she felt compelled to do something. This is just the way some mothers are. They rescue children—and adults! Rather than let the bride and groom be embarrassed, Mary did something. She turned to her firstborn for help. She knew her son; she figured He would help.

COUNTING ON JESUS

Mary didn't specifically ask Jesus to do anything. She simply looked at Him and said, "They are out of wine" (John 2:3). She expected Him to read her mind, and He did. Jesus readily understood what she wanted, and that's when He said something that makes me wince. He said, "Woman, what have I to do with thee?" (John 2:4 KJV).

Of course, He had something to do with her. He was her son! And why didn't He call her something more endearing such as Mother instead of Woman?

How could Jesus talk to His mother like that? Was Jesus being short with her or even rebuffing her? How could the wise, compassionate Jesus say something like this to His mother? Wouldn't this question have hurt her feelings? Wouldn't it have embarrassed her in front of family and friends?

And why wasn't He sympathetic to her concern for the wedding party? Since she cared, why didn't He care?

Apparently, Mary wasn't as bothered by His words as I was! She didn't become irritated or even mutter a verbal reply. Rather, she proceeded with confidence. She trusted Jesus to act. She said to the servants, "Do whatever Jesus tells you to do" (author's paraphrase), and they did!

Near the door there were six large water jars, placed there for ceremonial washings. "Jesus said to the servants, 'Fill these jars with water'" (John 2:7). The servants followed His instructions, and the water miraculously turned to wine. A wedding party was rescued. A young couple escaped embarrassment because Mary noticed, and Jesus responded.

I marvel that Mary didn't react with anger or defensiveness to Jesus' question. *Why*, I wondered, *was she able to calmly accept what Jesus said when I found His words offensive?*

5/21 ## A CULTURAL EXPLANATION

Calling someone Woman was quite acceptable in Jesus' day and time. It was both a normal and polite way of addressing women. Jesus used it on other occasions, with the Samaritan woman at the well (John 4:21), with a woman caught in adultery (John 8:10), with Mary again from the Cross (19:20), and with Mary Magdalene after His resurrection (20:13). Interestingly, when I read those incidents, I wasn't ever startled by Jesus' use of *woman,* and yet this wedding instance bothered me. Perhaps it's because Jesus followed "Woman . . ." with this question, "What have I to do with you?" If He had said, "Woman, how may I help?" I wouldn't have had a problem.

"What have I to do with you?" sounds as if He wanted to distance Himself from her, as if He felt "put off" by her request. Actually, the question is the Greek equivalent of a Hebrew idiom: "What to me and to you?" All cultures have idioms like this, and they sound awkward to people from another culture or another time. This often-quoted expression among Jews could be interpreted in two different ways.

1. When one party was unjustly bothering another, the injured party might say, "What to me and to you?" In other words, "What have I done to you that you should do this to me?" When it was used this way, some hostility was usually present.

2. But "What to me and to you?" was also used when there was some refusal of an ill-timed involvement or when there was a variance between the views of the two persons talking. It implies simple disengagement: "Your concern and mine are not the same."

In His way, with an idiomatic question, Jesus was trying to get Mary to understand their perspectives were different. Their concerns at the moment were not the same. I suggest this possibility because Jesus also said, "Mine hour is not yet come" (John 2:4 KJV).

ILL-TIMED INVOLVEMENT

Jesus often spoke of His *hour*. At first, when he used this word, it referred to His emergence as the deliverer (the Messiah) that God had promised His people. Later as His ministry evolved and intensified, the hour referred to His crucifixion and His death.

In His conversation with Mary, He was referring to the first meaning: His coming forward as the long-awaited deliverer. He was very much aware of the task His Father had sent Him to earth to do, and He was determined to do it, and to do His Father's way. This fulfillment of the Father's purpose was Jesus' "concern." He needed to weigh how any action might affect the proper unfolding of His entire mission. Would doing something about the wine hasten His hour?

So far Jesus had not performed any miracles, although He had preached and had enlisted a few disciples. When Jesus said, "My hour has not yet come," He was weighing whether this was the right time for this aspect of His nature to be revealed. This is the way *The Living Bible* interprets His words. "'I can't help you now,' he said. 'It isn't yet my time for miracles'" (John 2:4 TLB).

Mary's concern, on the other hand, was with the immediate situation. As a mother, as a homemaker, as one given to hospitality, she was thinking of the couple, the wedding, and the party.

Jesus and Mary were looking at this situation differently. Mary's thoughts were on the here and now—the occasion at hand—and Jesus' thoughts were on accomplishing God's overall will which would affect all of eternity.

Mary was going to have to understand that Jesus couldn't go on being the attentive, helpful son and at the same time be who the Father expected Him to be. Jesus' "what to me and to you?" may have been His way of saying, "Mother, you can't go on seeing Me as you have. My life is changing. Challenging times are ahead. Your life is changing too. I've been there for you personally, but now I have a wider mission ahead of Me. I need you to understand this."

About this time in my study Jesus spoke to me. Guess what He said.

"What to me and to you?"

With these words, Jesus reminded me that perspective matters. It matters in our relationship with others, and it matters in our relationship with Him.

Perspective facilitates conversations, working together, living together, and serving together. When we realize where another person is coming from or how they are seeing things, we can better understand them. It helps us know how to please others, and if need be, even be more intelligent in disagreeing with them.

I suspect perspective may have had something to do with my son seeing me as someone hard to talk with. He and his brother were on their way to becoming independent adults, both making mistakes and having victories along the way. I was seeing things from the perspective of "been there, done that." As a result of that process, I had developed strong convictions about what I perceived was the right and wrong way to live. While I wasn't communicating these convictions out loud (I knew better than that!), my facial expressions revealed my thoughts and feelings. Like Mary, I had to realize that times were changing and to adjust accordingly. I've been working at it ever since!

I also work at being conscious of Jesus' perspective; it's a discipline. I remember once disciplining myself to pray for others using the requests Jesus prayed for His disciples. What a difference this made!

5/24

PRAYING HIS PERSPECTIVE

I'll admit many of my prayers for others are "God, be with" and "God, help" prayers. Are yours?

I want comfort, security, and success for others. I think that's how I would have prayed for the disciples the night before Jesus' death. The hours ahead were going to be filled with trauma, shock, and grief for them. I would have prayed, "God, help them bear the shock. Comfort their hearts and help them to go on." But these are not the kinds of things Jesus asked for. While He was concerned for their immediate needs, His greater concern was that His work—the mission God gave Him to do—continued and expanded. For that the disciples would need unity, joy, protection, and dedication.

- *"Holy Father, keep them in Your name . . . that they may be one, even as We are"* (John 17:11 NASB). If the group became fragmented, God's work would be severely handicapped, perhaps stymied altogether, so Jesus prayed for them to be united.

- *"May [they] have the full measure of my joy within them"* (v. 13 NIV). Jesus had told the disciples that their values were different from the world's values; their standards were different from the world's standards. Consequently, they would be hated so Jesus wanted them to have joy (15:11; 16:24).

- *"My prayer is . . . that you protect them from the evil one"* (17:14–15 NIV). Satan would try to get His followers off course; therefore, Jesus prayed that God might protect them from the evil one. Being in the world was necessary for Jesus' disciples to complete His mission.

- *"Sanctify them by the truth; your word is truth"* (v. 17 NIV). Jesus prayed the disciples might be consecrated in God's Word just as He was being consecrated through His death on the Cross. He wanted them to serve without reservation.

For a while, I disciplined myself to pray these four requests for those on my prayer list. It was hard because the words didn't flow naturally, but I'm glad I prayed this way because I caught a glimpse of God's perspective. I got a bigger picture, one beyond the here and now. I could see the individuals as God might see them; I could imagine what He might want to achieve in their lives. He was doing something in their lives that had never occurred to me — something with eternal significance. This insight didn't mean I quit praying, but rather I prayed more fervently because I saw those for whom I was praying from an eternal perspective.

I'm not suggesting that we use these four prayer requests every day. Using them was a discipline, and our prayers often involve emotions, sometimes desperation, and the need for immediacy. We don't always have time to think through our prayer requests, and this is okay because the Bible says "Casting all your care upon him; for he careth for you" (1 Peter 5:7 KJV). But Jesus' words to Mary reminded me I might be doing too much "casting" without stopping to evaluate my requests from God's viewpoint. When Jesus said, "Woman, what have I to do with thee?" (John 2:4 KJV), He was reminding Mary — and me — that our concerns may not be the same as His concerns.

Because Jesus had a different perspective than Mary's didn't mean that He didn't care about the couple, the wedding party, and her request. His actions showed that He did. That's when the disciples also got a different perspective or maybe we should say an enlarged perspective of Jesus.

WHAT JESUS DID

After Jesus asked Mary the question about "what to me and to you?" Mary told the servants to do what He said. That's when Jesus said, "Fill these jars with water" (John 2:7).

The servants "filled them to the brim, and then he told them, 'Now draw some water out and take it to the man in charge of the feast" (vv. 7–8).

They did as Jesus asked and to everyone's surprise, the water was wine—very good wine. When he tasted it, the man in charge said, "Everyone else serves the best wine first, and after the guests have drunk a lot, he serves the ordinary wine. But you have kept the best wine until now!" (v. 10).

The six disciples who had been with Jesus only a short time had been watching this event transpire. They heard what Jesus said to the servants, they saw the servants comply with His instructions, and they heard the reaction of the man in charge. Clearly Jesus had performed a miracle, a miracle that "manifested His glory, and His disciples believed in Him" (v. 11 NASB).

Of course, they had been impressed with Him when they met Jesus in Judea or they wouldn't have fallen into step with Him. They experienced some interesting and thought-provoking conversations as they walked with Him. They recognized He was unusual (see John 1:48), but miracles? They had no idea of the extent of His supernatural ability.

At this point, their belief in Jesus solidified and grew. They deepened their commitment to Him. Their discipleship was evolving as all discipleship should, and as ours will, too, as we continue to look at what Jesus said to women. When we study what He said, we will grow in our knowledge of Him and His will. Our relationship will deepen, and we'll be more apt to see life and followship from His perspective.

FROM MIND TO HEART

What do you think was going through Mary's mind—what was she thinking and feeling—when she volunteered Jesus' help at this wedding? Did Mary expect Jesus to perform a miracle or do something else to solve the problem?

What does Mary's reaction tell us about Jesus' words, "Woman, what have I to do with thee?"

Has Jesus ever said anything to make you feel uncomfortable? Or to cause you to wince?

If it wasn't yet time for Jesus to reveal His supernatural ability to perform miracles, why do you suppose He took action?

Why does perspective matter?

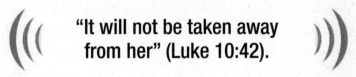

"It will not be taken away from her" (Luke 10:42).

YOU DON'T HAVE TO ATTEND CHURCH LONG BEFORE YOU BECOME familiar with Martha and Mary (Luke 10:38–42). Their story of how they responded to Jesus is referenced often. Martha invited Jesus to her home, and then became upset with her sister Mary. She sat serenely at Jesus' feet, listening to Him teach while Martha did all the work.

This story is so familiar among Christians that Martha has become a symbol—and sometimes a caricature—of women who get stressed out. Mary is held up as the ideal, as the truly spiritual woman.

Preachers, Bible study teachers, and speakers have been critical of Martha. I've been so bothered about this that before audiences, I jokingly claim to be president of the Martha Defense League. After all, Martha did some things right, and I make it a point to defend her beleaguered reputation. I'm a homemaker like her, and I've been known to lose my cool when entertaining just as she did, but that doesn't make me any less of a spiritual being. I also thrive on studying God's Word which is how this book came about. While "sitting at the feet of Jesus," I listened and heard what Jesus said to women. I discovered a surprise element in what He said. Now as we look at what He said to Martha, you may be thinking, *No surprise here,* because we know the words so well. Let's take a look at this familiar story and see. Did Jesus say anything surprising to Martha?

5/2⁷

MARTHA'S HOSTING

Martha lived in Bethany, a town near Jerusalem. Jesus was a celebrity, someone everyone was interested in because of His preaching, teaching, and healing. Wherever He went, crowds followed. This means He was almost always surrounded by noise and tension. Earlier Jesus had sent out 70 disciples into the villages and towns of Judea. Perhaps some of them told Martha about Jesus, adding to the stories she had already heard. She was intrigued, so when Jesus and His disciples came to Bethany, "Martha welcomed him in her home" (Luke 10:38).

Martha thought having Jesus in her home would be an opportunity to bring some refreshment to His life plus it would give her and her siblings a chance to know Him better. Her sister, Mary, and her brother, Lazarus, lived with her. They had all wondered if Jesus was really like people said He was.

But, even with the best of intentions, things don't always turn out the way you plan. Sometimes what you plan turns out to be more work than you anticipated which is what may have happened to Martha.

Among Jews, showing hospitality to a traveling teacher was a special privilege. Recognizing the importance of the occasion and Jesus' celebrity status, Martha wanted to do her best. She wanted to please Him so she began fixing lots of food, fluffing the cushions, looking for serving pieces, and finding a place for everyone to sit. But as the beads of perspiration started popping out on her forehead, it occurred to her that she was working alone.

No one stepped forth to help Martha. Where was Lazarus? And where was Mary? Martha really needed her sister, and she had assumed Mary, as Jewish women usually did, would help host Jesus and possibly the disciples too. Women in the same household usually worked together, but Mary wasn't helping. She was sitting at Jesus' feet, listening to him teach. Why was she not helping? This is when the "not fair" rule raised its ugly head.

WHAT'S THE "NOT FAIR" RULE?

It is the rule that resides in homes where there is more than one child. It is the rule that is present in the classroom. It is the rule that resides in the workplace and beyond. This rule is called on when something happens that makes a child—or an adult!—exclaim, "It's not fair."

As you take in what happens around you, as you observe who gets the favors, who gets the advantages, you recognize inconsistencies. The rewards of life are not being handed out equally. And it just isn't fair. The fury about this may be expressed in any number of ways.

- Why did I get the smaller half?
- Why don't you yell at her?
- Hey, it was my turn!
- Why can she eat anything she wants and not gain weight?
- Why does he always get the window seat?
- Why must I do all the work?

This last question must have been the one Martha asked herself. As Mary "sat down at the feet of the Lord and listened to his teaching" (Luke 10:39), Martha did all the work.

As we picture this scene, it would be easy to assume that Mary and Jesus were in the living room relaxing while Martha was stewing over a hot stove in the kitchen, but most Judean houses consisted of only one room, which served as living room, dining room, and bedroom. The cooking was done outside on an open fire. If this were the case, Martha would have had the frustration of trying to concentrate with people around her, hearing the teaching (teaching that she would have liked to have been a part of), and going in and out to tend to the fire. As thoughts of all *she* was responsible for and all that she was missing started rolling around in her head, she became "cumbered about much serving" (10:40 KJV).

In her frustration, Martha couldn't help but compare what Mary was getting and what she was getting from having company.

There was a big difference! Mary was enjoying herself, having the pleasure of Jesus' company and teaching, being fully absorbed, and Martha . . . well, she was doing all the work, and it just wasn't fair. Martha, in the heat of entertaining, appealed to Jesus to correct the unfairness.

THE APPEAL

Inherent in the "not fair" rule is the belief that someone, some person of authority (God, parent, boss, supervisor, etc.) can clear up the injustice and make things right. Martha didn't appeal to Mary, although Mary could have corrected the unfairness. She didn't say, "Mary, could you please help me, and then we can both sit at Jesus' feet and enjoy His company?"

No, Martha appealed to the One who should have noticed the discrepancy, to the One she was trying with so much effort to please. She appealed to Jesus. She said, "Lord, don't you care that my sister has left me to do all the work by myself? Tell her to come and help me!" (10:40).

When a child cries "unfair," he wants to know if the mother (or father) cares as much for him as she or he does his siblings. When a worker brings up the "not fair" rule to his boss, he wants to know, "Haven't you noticed how good (or how efficient) I've been?" He wants a pat on the back. When we see unfairness in the religious realm, when we're serving God, we want God to notice. We want to know that He's aware of us and that we have found favor with him.

Martha's appeal seems to indicate that the two sisters had started out working together as Jewish women would normally do. She said to Jesus, "My sister has left me to do all the work by myself." Mary had dropped the ball, leaving all the details and work to Martha, and planted herself as Jesus' feet. Martha had to carry on or no one was going to have anything to eat! This is simply not fair!

Her appeal included a solution: "Tell her to come and help me!" Anyone could see this was a reasonable and obvious action to take. If

Jesus would just tell Mary to help her, then Martha would have help and everything would be fair again. If anyone could equalize things, wouldn't Jesus be the one? Surely Jesus will make things right.

THE EXPECTED ANSWER

Jesus' answer to Martha is so well known to Christians that you may be scratching your head, wondering how His words are going to have a surprise element. But suppose you weren't a Christian. Or suppose you were hearing about Jesus' encounter with Martha for the first time, what would you assume Jesus would say in response to Martha's appeal?

I've written two Christmas books about Martha and Mary. One is *Can Martha Have a Mary Christmas?* and the other one is *Unwrapping Martha's Joy.* Those titles are fully comprehensible to Christian women—no explanation needed. When I'm talking with non-Christians, though, and these titles come up, I have to tell them the story of Martha and Mary to help them understand what the books are about. When I do, it's not unusual for a listener to ask, "Why didn't Jesus make Mary help Martha?"

One non-Christian woman from another country who knew something of Jesus, but not this story, interrupted me right before I got to Jesus' answer. She said, "Jesus told Mary to help, didn't He?"

She was anticipating that Jesus would render a fair verdict, that the work of hospitality would be shared by Mary and Martha so both could enjoy Jesus' company. But that's not what happened. Jesus didn't equalize the situation. He didn't reprimand Mary; instead he reprimanded Martha.

THE REPRIMAND

Jesus said, "Martha, Martha! You are worried and troubled over so many things, but just one is needed. Mary has chosen the right thing, and it will not be taken away from her" (Luke 10:41–42).

As president of the Martha Defense League, I think Martha should have received some commendation from Jesus. Some praise would have gone a long way in making things fairer than they were. Jesus could have expressed appreciation for her invitation and hard work. After all, she was the one who invited Him, a nervy thing for her to do since people were saying Jesus was *the* Messiah. Many persons interested in Him wouldn't have wanted to risk raising the ire of the religious leaders to host Jesus. Others may have felt like they didn't have lodging fit for a celebrity or couldn't furnish the food, but Martha opened her home to Him and His disciples. Shouldn't she have been commended for being willing to serve so many guests?

Or Jesus could have at least applauded her for seeing to the needs of her brother and sister. She was a protective sister to Lazarus and Mary, ensuring they were cared for. Perhaps if she hadn't provided domestic stability for Mary, she wouldn't have had the opportunity to sit at Jesus' feet.

While Jesus didn't commend her, He did speak affectionately to Martha. We can tell because He spoke her name twice ("Martha, Martha") the way parents do when they are exasperated yet amused at something their child is doing. With smiles on their faces, they shake their head in puzzlement, and say, "Sue, Sue, what are we going to do with you?"

His words also indicate that He had noticed. He said, "You are worried and troubled over so many things." So He had been paying attention! All that she was doing had not gone unnoticed. He was not indifferent to Martha's needs, yet He still reproved her because He had a lesson to teach her.

The lesson we most usually take from Jesus' words to Martha is about busyness. We shouldn't get so busy with "many things" when "just one thing is needed," that is, to focus on Jesus. While this is true—and important!—this is not how I understood His words.

GUESS WHAT HE SAID TO ME

Jesus' response to Martha's "not fair" appeal is not an excuse for Marys never to help in the kitchen or for Marthas not to study the Bible. Neither is His rebuke of Martha to imply that practical service is unimportant. Martha's service was important. On other occasions, Jesus had much to say about practical service, and the Bible has much to say about servanthood and hospitality.

But it was Jesus' words, "It will not be taken away from her" that gave me pause. Jesus wasn't going to answer Martha's accusation by taking away Mary's choice. Mary was still going to get to be Mary. She didn't have to stop doing what she was doing.

In other words, His role isn't making sure that all people who follow Him are treated equally. Blessing us isn't about catering to our sense of fairness on earth. Doing the Father's will is not about getting what we think we deserve; it's about choices and about coming to Him in light of our gifts, our personalities, and our circumstances.

If we didn't have comparative eyes, this would be a wonderful truth. We would be free to be ourselves, and to give our best to Him in light of who we are, not being forced to fit other molds. With comparative eyes, of which I have a keen set, we look at others and contrast what we have or don't have. And when we see a discrepancy, we cry, "Unfair," as Martha did.

Another biblical example that underscores this truth is when Jesus helps Peter come to grips with his having deserted Jesus after His arrest and denied knowing Him. Jesus loved Peter, though, and wanted to bring him back to a place where he could serve effectively. This had been Jesus' dream for Peter, but Peter had gotten off track. Peter needed to know he was forgiven and that Jesus had a work for him to do.

In their conversation, which is recorded in John 21:1–22, Jesus gave Peter work to do. He said, "Take care of my lambs" (v. 15) and "Take care of my sheep" (vv. 16, 17).

He also let Peter know what was ahead for him in the future when he was old. He would die a martyr's death. Peter didn't protest his future, but his comparative eyes circled around the other disciples standing nearby. They landed on John—who along with his brother James and Peter had formed Jesus' inner circle. Peter said, "Lord, what about John?"

In other words, if I am going to die for You, shouldn't John have to also? Why me? Why not him?

Jesus replied with an answer similar to the one He gave Martha.

Jesus said to Peter, "If I want him to live until I come, what is that to you?" (v. 22). Jesus did not provide a specific answer about John's fate. He denied Peter's request for specifics about John and urged him instead to focus on his own discipleship and service. He repeated what He had already said, "Follow me!" (vv. 19, 22).

Jesus doesn't need fairness to accomplish His will. He needs cooperation. He needs us to be who we are, to keep on following, which is exactly what both Peter and Martha did.

FOLLOWSHIP

Peter became the leader of the early church, preaching at Pentecost, boldly speaking of Jesus to the Jewish Sanhedrin, moving the gospel out beyond Judea into Samaria, raising Dorcas from the dead, and opening the door for Gentiles to become believers. Tradition is strong that Peter was arrested during Nero's persecution of Christians in Rome in AD 64–65 and subsequently crucified. There is additional tradition that he requested, and was permitted, to be crucified head downward because he did not feel worthy to die as Jesus had died.

Martha's outburst—her plea for fairness—didn't keep her from developing as a believer or keep her from serving again. She could have been ashamed of her emotional eruption and swore she wasn't going to get involved again. *Let someone else do the entertaining*. She could have been embarrassed by her behavior and concluded she never wanted to take any risks again. She could have been hurt by Jesus' remark and withdrawn emotionally from Him, but she didn't. She continued to serve well and grow spiritually as we'll see in a later chapter.

Peter and Martha's experiences help me understand that things aren't always "fair" in the Christian life. I appreciate the wisdom of this truth, but this doesn't mean I like applying the truth.

Interestingly, I had an exercise in application as I was writing this chapter. Another speaker was picked for an opportunity I thought was going to be mine. The event planner and I had been in the talking stage of planning for months. Then she ended up selecting a speaker she had never heard of and never met, just from a short blurb on the Internet. When she told me, I said to God, "I don't need a fresh exercise in applying the truth of this chapter!" But because I was writing, I didn't brood long about the perceived unfairness. I said to myself, "OK, Brenda, this isn't about fairness. This is about followship. Give up your feelings of unfairness and let them go," and that's what I did.

I realized then that the other speaker was the right fit for the event. I was acquainted with the speaker, and I knew she was exactly what the group needed. I thought, *The women are going to really enjoy her.*

Peace entered my heart and replaced the disgruntlement. I much prefer peace. That's why I'm thankful for the lesson I learned from Jesus' surprising words to Martha. It's also why I continue to serve as president of the Martha Defense League.

FROM MIND TO HEART

Which is better worship: sitting at the feet of Jesus or serving Jesus?

Did Jesus' response to Martha mean that serving is not important?

Even with the best of intentions, why is it easy for women who look after details of life to go into overdrive and miss what is most important? In what areas of the Christian life do you see this happening?

What are some occasions when you might perceive God as being unfair?

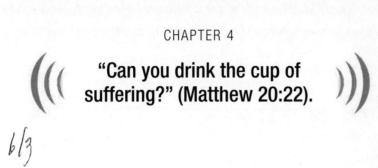 "Can you drink the cup of suffering?" (Matthew 20:22).

6/3

KYLIE, A WOMAN IN HER LATE 30s, IS A WIFE, A MOTHER OF FOUR children, and an active Christian. She works two jobs to help support her family. You can imagine how rushed she is to cover all her responsibilities. This was evident one morning as she arrived breathless and late to our Sunday School class. All eyes were on her as she entered the room. Slamming her Bible and quarterly down on the table, she said to the class, "What I want to know is, when do we get to 'happily ever after'?"

I said, "What?"

"You know," she said, "when does it all finally come together in the Christian life and you can breathe easy?"

The class chuckled thinking she was joking, but I knew she wasn't. Through the years of attending youth groups as a teenager, then women's Bible studies and Sunday School classes, she earnestly put into practice everything she learned. Somewhere along the way she picked up the idea that if she did everything right, the time would come when she would have a peaceful, orderly life.

This kind of thinking happens to many of us, not that we all arrive at the same conclusion! Putting together in our heads what we hear and see, we arrive at an expectation about life. This expectation influences how we live, but the day may come when we are forced to reconsider. This is what happened to Salome. In midlife, an expectation developed in her mind that she was absolutely certain would come to pass, and her adult sons agreed with her. A conversation with Jesus, though, forced her to revaluate what she believed.

6/4 WHO WAS SALOME?

Salome was the wife of Zebedee, the owner of a fishing business. He and Salome had two adult sons, James and John, also known as the "sons of thunder." This makes you wonder if Zebedee was loud, overbearing, and obnoxious or if the sons were always being loud, getting angry, or acting impulsively?

Zebedee's business had done so well that he had hired workers to help. James and John's friend, Simon Peter, also a fisherman, merged his work with theirs from time to time. He was there the day Salome decided to take time out from her work to watch them handle their fishing nets near Lake Gennesaret. As she stood watching, she first heard and then saw a crowd of people walking along the shoreline.

As they got closer, she saw her sister's son, Jesus, leading the group and speaking to them. *Oh, oh, did this mean James and John might leave again?* Once they had followed Jesus in Judea for a while and had since returned home. Selfishly, she hoped they would stay. Their presence was a comfort to her and Zebedee.

She moved closer to the people to hear Jesus speak. His voice was compelling, making her want to keep listening. His words were powerful, like nothing she had ever heard. She could understand why people wanted to hear more.

As people pushed to get closer to Jesus, He got into one of Simon's boats. He said, "Push off a little from the shore." Then He sat in the boat and resumed teaching the crowd.

When Jesus finished speaking, He challenged Simon, "Push the boat out further to the deep water, and . . . let down your nets" (Luke 5:4). Peter balked at first, but then he did it anyway. He caught so many fish that the nets were about to break.

Peter was aghast at the catch. "He fell on his knees before Jesus and said, 'Go away from me, Lord! I am a sinful man!'" (v. 8).

Then Jesus said to all of them, "Don't be afraid; from now on you will be catching people" (vv. 9–11).

Catching men? Salome wondered, *What did Jesus mean?*

Apparently Peter, James, and John knew. "They pulled the boats up on the beach, left everything, and followed Jesus" (v. 11). Just like that, her sons were gone. She wondered, What kind of hold did Jesus have over them that prompted James, John and Peter to drop everything and go with Him? Did they know what they were doing?

NOW WHAT?

There was so much about Jesus that Salome didn't know, and yet every day she and Zebedee heard about Jesus from customers. They heard how He healed people, exorcized demons, defied the religious leaders, and attracted large crowds. The more Salome heard, the more intrigued she became. She said to Zebedee, "I want to go see James and John. I have to know what is going on."

Zebedee may have been unhappy with her decision. From now on in the Bible, she is referred to as the *mother* of Zebedee's children and not as the *wife* of Zebedee (or this could have meant that he had died).

On the other hand, Zebedee could have been very supportive. He might have said, "I'll stay here and run the business. You go and help Jesus. Take some money with you. I imagine Jesus, James, John, and Peter are going to need some financial support." I say this because Salome became a part of a group of Galilean women who traveled with Jesus and the apostles. This group supported them out of their "substance" (Luke 8:3 KJV) or "resources." In other words, they supported Jesus financially.[1]

As Salome traveled with Jesus, the apostles, and the other women, she listened to what Jesus said and to what others said about Him. Mingling in the crowds, she quickly learned many people were seeing Jesus as the promised Messiah. All through their history, the Jews had dreamed of the Messiah—a conqueror, a mighty leader, one who would smash the enemies of Israel, and reign in power over the kingdoms of the earth. Salome found herself agreeing with them. *Yes, indeed, He's the one!*

In her mind's eye, she could see the establishment of an earthly kingdom with Jesus as the head. Jesus would deliver the Jews by taking charge, defeating the Romans, and putting them in control of the government. This image became more powerful day by day, and she fully expected it to happen.

As she reveled in this expectation, her mental wheels turned. If Jesus was their mighty deliverer, if He defeated the Romans, if He established a kingdom here, He would be the Head. If He were the Head, then He would have assistants. These assistants would occupy powerful and honorable positions, so what do you think occurred to Salome?

JESUS, WHAT ABOUT MY SONS?

Salome had noted how Jesus had regarded James, John, and Peter as His closest comrades. He relied on them in a way that was different from how he related to the other apostles. Surely, this meant He would be favorable for making them His highest assistants. She beamed as she thought of James and John occupying powerful positions in Jesus' established kingdom.

At first she kept this idea to herself, but this proved to be too much. She started hinting of the possibility to James and John. Then with her excitement building, she told them what she was thinking. They responded, "Aw, Mom," like the whole idea totally embarrassed them. It wasn't long, though, before they admitted the idea appealed to them too.[2]

They might have kept this idea to themselves if an ominous cloud of impending doom hadn't descended on the camp. The women could tell something was up. The women weren't always privy to everything Jesus said so they didn't know He had warned His disciples about His going to Jerusalem and being killed.[3] They just sensed danger ahead. So the women decided to follow Jesus to Jerusalem in Judea, where they usually didn't travel with Him.

Salome wondered if this sense of impending doom meant things were coming to a head, that Jesus would declare His power and establish His kingdom. In her mind's eye, she could see Him riding into Jerusalem as a conquering hero, taking over the Roman government and putting Himself in charge. Fully believing Jesus was going to reveal His military prowess, Salome said to James and John, "Guys, it's time we talked with Jesus."

6/7   THE "TALK"

Salome went to Jesus "with her sons, worshipping him, and desiring a certain thing of him" (Matthew 20:20 KJV). "Worshipping him" doesn't mean that she humbly approached Jesus with a heart full of adoration and praise. More probably it meant she bowed before Him as if she were petitioning an earthly king which is what she expected Him to be. Her kneeling was part of her strategy to influence Jesus, to make her case stronger because she wanted "a certain thing of him."

What was that "certain thing?" That's what Jesus wanted to know. He asked, "What do you want?" (v. 21).

His question forced Salome to clarify her desire, and she did without hesitation. She came right out with what she wanted. She said, "When You get your kingdom established, give my two sons the thrones on either side of you. Place one on the right hand, and the other on your left."

Some people in today's aggressive culture might applaud Salome for what she did. She knew what she wanted and she moved forward to get it. She was being a good mother, and her sons certainly didn't object. In Mark's account, they say to Jesus, "There is something we want you to do for us" (10:35).

Jesus' reply was as blunt as Salome's request was aggressive. There was no "I understand, Salome, where you are coming from" or "You really care for your sons, don't you?" He said, "You don't know what you're asking for" (Matthew 20:22).

Salome bristled. She knew very well what she was asking! She had nursed her idea for weeks. This was no spur of the moment whim. Her sons were capable men, and they could be of help to Jesus. Jesus would have many responsibilities once He became the head of Palestine, if not the Roman Empire. As remarkable as He was, Jesus would still need help. Any leader does. Her sons were just the ones who could capably assist Him. What else was there to know?

She wanted to say, "I beg your pardon," but she didn't. She wanted to defend her request, but some kind of check in her inner spirit prompted her to remain quiet.

Jesus, though, didn't. He went on speaking. He asked, "Can you drink the cup of suffering that I am about to drink?" (v. 22).

A cup of suffering? What was that?

Salome needed to know, and so do we if we want to have a clearer picture of what following Him means.

THE CUP OF SUFFERING

If we study Jesus' question as it appears in the King James Version, we can get a fuller understanding of what Jesus meant. In this version, Jesus says, "Are ye able to drink of the cup that I shall drink of, and to be baptized with the baptism that I am baptized with?" (Matthew 20:22 KJV).

This "cup" could be a metaphor for both life and death. If it represents life, then it could refer to the persistent struggle and discipline necessary to deal with suffering in this life, particularly the heartbreaks, hurts, and disappointments that occur because we are believers. If cup represents death, then "drinking" it would mean dying because you believe in and follow Jesus.

Being baptized means being submerged in something such as being submerged in paperwork or submerged in questions. It could also mean being submerged in certain emotions such as grief, fear, and worry. Maybe you have felt yourself submerged and close to drowning when watching a loved one suffer. You were experiencing a baptism of sorrow and helplessness.

By His questions then, Jesus was saying, "Can you endure suffering as My followers? Can you endure hard times? Are you willing to be submerged in hatred and pain? Can you give your life for Me if necessary?" To drink the cup of suffering means following Christ, going where He leads, and striving to be like Him in any situation. This doesn't mean we all drink the exact same cup, but it does mean that we can all expect to suffer at some time or other if we are true believers.

As she comprehended what Jesus was saying, Salome felt weak. Suffering wasn't something she wanted for her sons. She hadn't expected an answer like this. Apparently her sons didn't either because they quickly said, "Yes, we can," to Jesus' question, "Can you drink the cup of suffering?" Their answer was too quick, as if they didn't catch the full effect of what Jesus was saying. Perhaps that's why Jesus immediately said, "You will indeed drink from my cup" (v. 23). He was making Himself clear that suffering was to come — for Him and His followers.

TO DRINK OR NOT TO DRINK

The thought of her sons suffering and possibly being martyred could have caused Salome to throw up her hands in defeat and say, "That's it! I had no idea following Jesus meant suffering. Jesus was right when He said I didn't know what I was asking. Knowing what I do now, I simply can't follow Him any longer. I'm going home, and I wish James and John would come home too."

Even though Jesus hadn't traveled outside Palestine, stories of His miracle-working abilities had. Once someone spotted Him, word spread letting people know the miracle worker was in town. They gathered around the house where Jesus was staying. One person, a Gentile woman, bolder than the others, pushed her way through the crowd and into the house. She was not only an interruption; her behavior was uncouth and rowdy.

The Bible describes this woman as a Syrophoenician, a Greek, and a Canaanite. How's that possible? Tyre and Sidon were in Syria where Mediterranean coastal cities to the north of Israel had been—the location of ancient Phoenicia—hence, she's called the Syrophoenician woman. She spoke Greek as most people throughout the Roman Empire did so Mark refers to her as "Greek" (Mark 7:26 NIV), or "Gentile" (NIV). Matthew, who wrote for Jews, called her a "Canaanite" (15:22 NIV), linking her with those who occupied Canaan when it was promised to Abraham hundreds of years earlier. The descendants of the Canaanites were often spoken of with reproach in the Old Testament. Mentioning that she was Canaanite was Matthew's way of letting us know that of all people, this woman should *not* be approaching a Jew for help. She did, though. She sought Jesus' help, not for herself but for her daughter.

Her daughter, who was not with her, was "grievously vexed with a devil" (KJV). In other words she was suffering terribly from the work of a demon, also known as an evil spirit or an unclean spirit. It's hard to say exactly what the girl's symptoms were. In some people, the work of a demon affected sight and speech. "Some people brought to Jesus a man who was blind and could not talk because he had a demon" (12:22). Others who were possessed spoke audibly but strangely. Some afflicted with demons screamed (1:26; 5:5).

Strange behavior was characteristic of some who were demon possessed. The Gerasene demonic "wandered among the tombs and through the hills, screaming and cutting himself with stones" (5:5). A boy possessed by an evil spirit foamed at the mouth, gritted his teeth, and became stiff all over (9:18). One boy had such terrible attacks that he often fell in the fire or into water (Matthew 17:15).

What mother wouldn't be distraught if her child displayed any of these symptoms? No wonder the Syrophenician woman wanted help for her suffering daughter. Perhaps she had already sought help from exorcists in her area. Exorcists were prevalent because there was such a pervasive belief in demons. They used elaborate incantations, spells, and magical rites to drive our demons. That's why the people in Capernaum of Galilee were impressed with Jesus when earlier in His ministry He had exorcised a demon with a word of authority.[2] No one had seen anything like it! Perhaps this is one of the stories about Jesus that fanned out into Gentile country. When the Syrophenician woman heard it, she wished her daughter could benefit from Jesus' help. And now, Jesus was here in her area! If she could get to Jesus and talk to Him, she believed He would heal her daughter!

She found the house and pushed her way through the crowd and through the door. Once inside, she loudly cried, "Have mercy on me, O Lord, thou Son of David; my daughter is grievously vexed with a devil" (15:22 KJV). It wasn't the mannerly thing to do, it wasn't the reasonable thing to do, but by being pushy, she got into the house where Jesus and His disciples were retreating.

SURPRISE #3: JESUS' SILENCE

Once she was in Jesus' presence, once He saw how distraught she was, wouldn't you expect Jesus to readily help? Here was a hurting mother. She was seeking help for her "little daughter" (Mark 7:25 NIV). Even if she were going about it in an unmannerly way, her intention was admirable and understandable. She was seeking help for her child. Wouldn't Jesus who loved children and welcomed them in His presence (see Mark 10:13–16) have a heart for a hurting child, especially one that was grievously vexed with a devil? Wouldn't He readily help?

He didn't, though. Instead, "He answered her not a word" (Matthew 15:23 KJV). Why didn't He say to the woman, "Come on in. Tell me what's bothering you. Let me know how I can help." Wouldn't this have been the compassionate approach? The kind thing to do?

But this is not what happened. He didn't even acknowledge her presence. Instead, He spoke to the disciples, and what He said puzzled me even further.

SURPRISE #4: WHAT HE SAID TO THE DISCIPLES

Jesus was aware of the commotion, of the woman's noisy entrance. He could hear her loud cries. He didn't say anything, but His disciples did. They urged Jesus to give her whatever she wanted. They said, "Send her away, for she keeps crying out after us" (Matthew 15:23 NIV). She was a nuisance to the disciples. This Gentile woman had come unbidden into a place where she hadn't been invited. Actually, according to their culture, she had no right to expect help from a Jew. She had no right to even be speaking directly to Jewish males. She should have had a male (her husband, father, or brother) to intercede on her behalf. She hadn't been invited to be a part of their meeting, so their attitude was, *Give her what she wants, so we can get rid of her.*

When they said as much, Jesus broke His silence. He looked at them and said, "I was sent only to the lost sheep of Israel" (v. 24 NIV). "The lost sheep of Israel" were the Jews. How offensive this must have sounded to her! How offensive this sounds to twenty-first-century ears when we are continually reminded to include everyone and not be separatists. If not offensive to twenty-first-century ears, then it is to the ears of Christians who have a heart for missions. We believe in going into the entire world with the gospel. We want every group of people to hear the gospel. We believe the words of the Apostle Paul: "There is no difference between Jews and Gentiles" (Galatians 3:28).

In this small, crowded house, the woman couldn't help but hear Jesus' statement to the disciples. If I were her, I would have been totally discouraged at this point. I would have quietly backed out the door and gone home defeated. I'm a give-up-and-accept type of person. But not her; she pressed on.

She had no reason to think that Jesus, a Jew, would listen to a Canaanite, but she appealed to Him anyway. Her daughter's life was at stake, so she fell down before Jesus and said, "Help me, sir!" (Matthew 15:25).

Now, here, surely Jesus will be sympathetic. This mother is desperately pleading, having no shame, throwing herself on His mercy, and I'm ready for Him to show some mercy, aren't you? I want to believe that Jesus responds to mothers. I want to believe that He would care for demon-possessed children, that He would want to set them free. Instead Jesus makes a puzzling statement about dogs.

SURPRISE #5: DOES JESUS CALL HER A DOG?!

Jesus said to her, "It isn't right to take the children's food and throw it to the dogs" (Matthew 15:26).

Since these words follow His statement, "I was sent only to the lost sheep of Israel," the implication is that the "children" are the Jews (the "lost sheep of Israel") and the "dogs" are the Gentiles. The Jews at that time thought of Gentiles as dogs, and the Gentiles didn't feel much better about the Jews. They held each other in contempt.

His words sound to me like Jesus was calling her a dog! I was relieved to learn that He was making a comparison that would communicate a valuable message in the context of His culture. Jews had two cultural words for dog: *pariah* and *kunaria*. *Pariah* were the wild, often rabid, street dogs that everyone feared and avoided. *Kunaria* were the pet dogs people kept in their homes. Jesus didn't use the word for street dogs, which would have indeed been an insult. Contrastingly, Jesus used the more affectionate word *kunaria*; therefore, "we can be quite sure that the smile on Jesus' face and the compassion in His eyes robbed the words of all insult and bitterness."[3]

Nevertheless, His words gave the Gentile woman the impression that Jesus could and would only help Jews. This did not discourage her, though. She did not get her feelings hurt as some Pharisees did when Jesus said something unsettling to them (see Matthew verses 11–12). Instead she retorted with words that delighted Jesus.

SURPRISE #6: THE WOMAN'S RETORT

She picked up on Jesus' choice of words, and used them in a counter argument. "'Yes it is, Lord,' she said, 'Even the dogs eat the crumbs that fall from their master's table'" (Matthew 15:27 NIV). Mentally, she matched Jesus thought for thought. Her implied message was, "Can't you throw some crumbs my way now?"

According to Dwight L. Moody, she was saying something like this: "'Yes, Lord, I acknowledge I am a Gentile dog; but I remember that even the dogs have some privileges, and when the door is open they slink in and crawl under the table. When the bread or the meat sifts through the cracks of the table or falls off the edge of it, they pick it up, and the master of the house is not angry with them. I do not ask for a big loaf; I do not ask even for a big slice; I only ask for that which drops down through the chinks of the table—the dogs' portion. I ask only the crumbs.'"[4]

Her bright, forceful, and intelligent answer impressed Jesus, and so did her courage. He appreciated the fact that she was a Gentile woman speaking up and matching the mind of a Jewish male. And not just any Jewish male! He was aware of His reputation as a miracle worker, a possible political Messiah, an authoritative teacher, and an exorcist. Many women would have been intimidated by Him, but this woman wasn't. She was not afraid to converse with Him. (While we may be aghast that she would actually talk to Jesus this way, we must remember that she likely did not think He was divine. In her view,

He was a healer and an exorcist, and she was a determined mother.)

Her motive in answering Jesus wasn't to show Him up, to embarrass Him, or to reveal how smart she was. Her reply was born out of love. She persevered and spoke up because she was seeking help for her terribly disturbed daughter.

Jesus was not shocked or put off by her answer. Rather He complimented her faith.

SURPRISE #7: JESUS' DELIGHT

Jesus answered her retort with a compliment. And what a compliment it was! He said, "Woman, you have great faith!" (Matthew 15:28 NIV). He didn't say, "You have some faith" or "a little faith" or "just enough faith." Rather He said she had "great faith." In our English translations, this compliment is followed by an exclamation mark, indicating the forcefulness of His expression.

Isn't this amazing? If you were taught to "sit still," "be quiet," "mind your manners," and "don't interrupt," then surely you are puzzled by Jesus' praising a woman who interrupted a meeting, spoke her mind, challenged His words, and persisted in what she wanted. Shouldn't praise go to good, well-behaved people?

Goodness does have its rewards, but there's also joy in seeing hidden qualities in individuals come to light. A teacher may have this kind of experience. She believes behind that brusque outer behavior or underneath that inability to sit still is a child with potential. She may prod him, give him an unusual assignment, have him change seats, make some reactionary statement to him, or any number of other things that will crack the surface and allow his hidden potential to surface. Oh, what joy for the teacher when this happens!

Jesus was a Master Teacher and perhaps His silence, His startling statements, and His refusal to respond immediately were His ways of getting the woman's faith to shine. Underneath the woman's uncouth, loud behavior was stellar faith. And when it surfaced, He was delighted. He saw in her what the disciples missed seeing—remarkable faith. Jesus not only praised her, He rewarded her. He said, "What you want will be done for you" (v. 28). He set the daughter free from demon possession even though the girl was not in His presence. When the Gentile woman went home, she "found her child lying on the bed, and the demon gone" (Mark 7:30 NIV). Her mission was accomplished.

The woman got what she wanted, so is Jesus saying to us that if we're obnoxious, rude, and talk back to Him we will get what we ask? No, that's not what He's saying. As we are seeing—and will continue to see—women approach Jesus in various ways. Some women are bold, some are shy, and others are somewhere in between.

What He is saying is this: "Don't hesitate to approach Me. Come to Me as you are. State your case before Me if you are in need of something. If you can't articulate your case well, don't worry about it. I will help you.[5] I may make conversation with you as I did with the Syrophoenician woman. Some of My words may be a little shocking but they will cause what faith you have to burn brightly. All that's needed for you to approach Me is to believe that I'm real and that I reward those who seek Me. This approach is what pleases Me.[6] And who knows? I may be so delighted that I will say to you as I said to the Syrophoenician woman, 'Woman, you have great faith!'"

FROM MIND TO HEART

How do you approach Jesus—with confidence or timidity? Or does your approach depend on your need at the time?

What action would it take on our part to hear a word of commendation from Jesus?

What kind of faith pleases God?

What motivated the Gentile woman's faith? Was her faith perfect? Is perfect faith necessary to having Jesus respond to us?

How is this woman like Salome? How is she not like her?

Why is it surprising that Jesus complimented the woman's faith?

What does this incident tell us about Jesus?

What's Jesus saying to us through this incident?

"How lucky are the women who never had children" (Luke 23:29).

I CAN'T REMEMBER A TIME WHEN I DIDN'T WANT TO BE A MOTHER. Perhaps there was such a moment before I started playing with dolls, but I can't recall it. I enjoyed "mothering" my dolls in the playhouse that my sisters and I shared. I also enjoyed lining up the dolls and teaching them before I moved on to teaching "live" children, first at church and then in high school. In my second year of teaching, I said to my mother, "I'm tired of working with other people's children. I want my own." I didn't want life to pass without getting to be a mother. I realize not all women feel this way, but I share this about myself so you will see why I was so puzzled by something Jesus said. He said there would be a time when women who never had children would be lucky. Lucky? How could they be lucky?

With God orchestrating our lives, we Christians don't usually think in terms of luck. The King James Version uses the word "blessed," and I think that's preferable. Biblical women certainly considered themselves blessed to be mothers. As Ray Summers says in his Commentary on Luke, "Bearing children was the most exalted privilege of womanhood."[1] For a woman not to be able to have children was considered a curse. There was no tragedy like a childless marriage; in fact, childlessness was a valid ground for divorce. And yet Jesus speaks of a time when not to have children would be a blessing. Why would Jesus say such a thing?

WHEN JESUS SAID THIS

When Jesus said, "How lucky are the women who never had children" (Luke 23:29), He was on the way to the Cross. Literally. While He had made references to His dying in His teaching and preaching, the time had actually come. During His ministry, opposition from the Jews had developed against Him and increased to the point that He was arrested in Jerusalem during Passover. After His arrest late Thursday evening, He was subjected to several "trials" throughout the night and into early Friday morning. He appeared three times before the Jews and then three times before Roman authorities. During this time, He was taunted, probed, questioned, mocked, slapped, and scourged, and then the Roman-appointed governor, Pontius Pilate, sentenced Jesus to die.

Pilate immediately turned Jesus over to Roman soldiers to carry out the execution. The soldiers led Jesus away, moving Him toward the crucifixion site. Two other men, two criminals, were being crucified along with Him. According to custom, each person had to carry his own cross. Boxed around each cross-carrying criminal were four soldiers. Another soldier walked in front of the "box" carrying a sign that declared the person's crime. This procession of criminals and guards took the longest route possible to the crucifixion site outside Jerusalem as a graphic way to deter crime. Along the route, they attracted followers. In this case, "A large crowd of people followed" (v. 27). The throng included quite a mixture.

- The High Priests who engineered Jesus' arrest, their servants, and other Jews who had been intent on bringing about Jesus' death. In their eyes, they had won, but they wanted to make sure. They wanted to witness His demise.

- Jews who lived in Jerusalem and those in town for the Passover. Many were aware of Jesus, His reputation, and the hostility toward Him; others not as knowledgeable but still interested in what was happening.

- Family members and friends of the criminals who didn't want their loved ones to die alone.
- Rabble-rousers from the streets and curious spectators, people drawn to the drama of the latest execution.
- There were also women in the crowd.

These women were the "Daughters of Jerusalem" (v. 28 KJV), residents of Jerusalem who took pride in their Jewish history and being citizens of Jerusalem. As the crowd moved toward Golgotha, the crucifixion site on a hill outside the city walls, these women were grieved by what was happening right before their eyes, right in their treasured city.

WHAT THEY SAW

The Daughters of Jerusalem noticed that Jesus was getting weary. His energy was depleted from all He had been through that week. It had been one of intense strain, followed by the tension of the trials, the brutal scourging, and the repeated mockery.

The soldiers, too, recognized His weariness. They got help for Him when they met Simon, a man from Cyrene, who was coming into Jerusalem. The soldiers "seized him, put the cross on him, and made him carry it behind Jesus" (Luke 23:26).

While this slightly relieved the women's concern, they still hurt for Jesus. They could see the strain He was under and thought of how He must be in pain from the scourging. And, too, they couldn't stop thinking about His innocence. While they weren't privy to everything going on in Jerusalem, they did know Jesus wasn't guilty of any crime like the other two men, and yet He was being put to death. He had already suffered much, and He would suffer more on the Cross. The Crucifixion and its awfulness was something everyone was familiar with because the Romans crucified so many slaves and criminals.

The women took all this in: the weariness on Jesus' face, Simon's having to carry His cross, the broken skin where the scourging whip had struck repeatedly, and the blood running down His face and back. At the same time, they worried about the excruciating, painful death that was ahead for Him. Consequently, they did what any self-respecting, sensitive woman would do; they cried. Wouldn't you? I know I would have.

WEEPING WOMEN

Many women have a sensitive, empathetic nature. We can readily identify with the pain of others and are easily moved to tears. I don't even have to know the people in order to cry. Television scenes of hurting people halfway around the world—people I've never met and have no connection with—will prompt tears to run down my cheeks.

The weeping, though, of the Daughters of Jerusalem was not gentle tears surfacing, spilling out, and slipping down their cheeks. These women lamented, crying loudly, and beating their grief-stricken breasts. Loud vocal grief demonstrations like this were customary in their day. Public wailing over the dying or other tragedies meant anguished crying, pulling out hair, and even clawing the face with fingernails.

Hearing their wailing and observing their behavior, Jesus said to them, "Women of Jerusalem! Don't cry for me, but for yourselves and your children. For the days are coming when people will say, 'How lucky are the women who never had children, who never bore babies, who never nursed them!' That will be the time when people will say to the mountains, 'Fall on us!' and to the hills, 'Hide us!' For if such things as these are done when the wood is green, what will happen when it is dry?" (Luke 23:28–31).

Jesus said, "Don't cry for me," because mourning for Him was not needed. He was doing God's will, and God was helping Him endure. Throughout the previous three years, Jesus had prayed and communed with God about His future. From time to time, He wrestled with His destiny, but the final battle had been won just hours earlier in the Garden of Gethsemane. God had strengthened and prepared Him. Now Jesus had the inner resolve and strength to do what was necessary. This didn't mean dying would be easy or He wouldn't suffer, but it did mean He would be triumphant and that a purpose was being served.

The Daughters of Jerusalem were looking at what they saw right before their eyes, never considering an eternal perspective. They saw a distraught, weary Jesus on the way to a death He didn't deserve. They saw a man who was suffering and would soon suffer even more. The customary thing to do at a time like this was weep and wail. They didn't realize that Jesus was carrying out the redemptive purposes of God.

To redirect their grief, Jesus instructed them to cry for themselves and their children. The women were surprised by this. They thought they were doing the appropriate thing. What Jesus knew, though, and they didn't was that worse days were coming.

"FOR THE DAYS ARE COMING . . ."

A time was coming when women who never had children, who never bore babies, and who never nursed them would be considered fortunate. They would be glad that they hadn't tasted of motherhood in any way. The heartache would be great for women who had carried children in their wombs, nursed them, and formed strong attachments with them. The emotional pain these mothers would experience would be almost unbearable. That's when women who hadn't experienced motherhood would be lucky!

When these "days" arrive, the destruction from conflict and fighting would be so terrible that people would "say to the mountains, 'Fall on us!'" and to the hills, 'Hide us!'" (Luke 23:30). What they experienced would be so horrendous that people would long for natural calamities. Being quickly crushed to death by falling rocks and dirt would be preferable to the prolonged agony of dying at the hands of men.

The women hushed at Jesus' sobering words and stared at Him with a "you've got to be kidding" look. In their heads, they were thinking: *Our culture values children, motherhood is a blessing, we are good citizens of Jerusalem, we are godly women, the Romans treat us well, the Temple is here, and we are God's people. He won't let anything like this happen here.*

Jesus, though, emphasized the certainty of what would happen by comparing green wood and dry wood. He said, "For if such things as these are done when the wood is green, what will happen when it is dry?" (v. 31). The New International Version says, "For if people do these things when the tree is green, what will happen when it is dry?" Green wood (or a green tree) is hard to burn, and dry wood burns readily.

In making this contrast, *Jesus might have been referring to the Romans*. If the Romans dealt with Jesus, whom they considered innocent, by executing Him, how much worse would they deal with guilty and rebellious people in the future? If they treated someone who wasn't guilty by crucifying Him, what would they do to those who deserved punishment?

Or *Jesus could have been referring to Jerusalem Jews*. God's favor was extended to them when He offered them His Son as their Messiah ("when the tree is green"), but they rejected His overtures. Consequently, a day of no opportunity (dry wood) would come when God's favor would not be extended to them. Jesus had warned Jerusalem about this just a few days earlier. He said, "The days will come upon you when your enemies build an embankment against you and encircle you and hem you in on every side. They will dash you to the ground, you and the children within your walls. They will not leave one stone on another, *because you did not recognize the time of God's coming to you*" (Luke 19:43–44 NIV; author's italics). Actually, both of these possibilities became realities when the "coming days" arrived.

WHEN THE WOOD WAS DRY

When Jesus said what He did to the Daughters of Jerusalem, some Jews were chafing against the Roman government. They resented being under their control even though the Romans allowed them much leeway living the way they wanted and in practicing their religion. Still, some Jews were actively resentful. Eventually their disgruntlement grew into full-blown rebellion, and other Jews joined them. The Roman armies moved in to squelch it.

The Jews weren't united in their opposition. If they had been, they might have been able to fight back successfully. They couldn't agree on issues and methods. This divided them into factions and weakened them. Often they were more intent on attacking one another than fighting the Romans. The Jews killed each other's men and destroyed one another's food supplies. Jerusalem's children were snatched from their mothers and slaughtered before their eyes. Talk about a reason to weep and to wail!

The Temple was set on fire. Accounts vary on how this fire got started, but the blaze swelled, spread, and consumed building after building until Jerusalem was destroyed. As you picture this, can't you see why people would cry out for the mountains to fall on them? Being instantly destroyed by a huge boulder or a landslide would be much preferred over being burned to death.

Even though the Jews saw themselves as God's people, He did not rush into rescue them. Their day of opportunity had passed. Judgment had arrived. Over 1,100,000 people perished before the war was over in AD 70, and 97,000 Jews were carried away into captivity. This is when the Jewish nation with its center in Jerusalem ceased to exist[2] and the sacrificial system ended.

This bit of history helped me understand why Jesus would say, "How lucky are the women who never had children" to the Daughters of Jerusalem. But I also wanted to know if His words had something to say to Daughters of Today?

6/23

GUESS WHAT HE SAID TO ME

As I meditated on what Jesus said to the Daughters of Jerusalem, I heard Him say three things.

Be alert to what grieves you. The Daughters of Jerusalem were upset about what was happening to Jesus and mourned loudly. And yet Jesus told them, "Don't pray for me." He wanted them to redirect their grief to where it was really needed.

At times, some of us may need to do some redirecting. For example, we can ring our hands, cry, moan, and get bent out of shape about what we think is necessary for a better, safer, healthier, and more comfortable life and yet fail to get upset over spiritual concerns. I thought of this when for several weeks I attended a small, what appeared to be dying church. They had more than 100 people on their prayer list, and they meticulously went over this list every Sunday in the worship service. Almost all their concerns were physical needs—hemorrhoid surgery, back trouble, and even the common cold. The Sunday a woman wanted to be added to the list because she was having a routine colonoscopy, I wanted to say, "Get a grip, folks. You will always have physical ailments. You may not always have a church, though, if you don't start focusing your worship on God."

I understand wanting others to pray with us about our concerns—and even recommend this—but I also think it's wise to periodically evaluate what grieves us. Two things help me with this: (1) Keeping a prayer journal. Occasionally as I thumb back through the pages, I realize I'm getting self-centered. That's when I make a deliberate effort to get back on track praying for others. (2) Belonging to a missions organization where I am continually reminded to think globally. Honoring God means caring about the whole world.

Be conscious that life isn't lived on a plane. On this side of the Cross, knowing God's will was for Jesus to die for our sins, we often have a simplistic, demystified view of His death. Jesus came, He lived, He died, God's purpose was fulfilled, and that was that. Yet people were involved. There were choices. There were decisive actions. There were consequences. There was judgment. The early church in Jerusalem saw the Jews as guilty for bringing about the death of Jesus even though they also saw it as God's plan and as a fulfillment of prophecy (Acts 2:23, 36; 3:13–15; 4:10; and 5:30). Life isn't lived on a simple plane. It's more 3-D than 2-D or 1-D (one-dimensional). Life is complex.

Remember there's more going on than what we can see. We may be so grieved by the dynamics of what we're involved in and what is going on around us that we become just as distressed as the Daughters of Jerusalem. At the same time, even though they couldn't see it, God was moving. Through it all, He was accomplishing His redemptive purpose.

I think about this when I sit on my front porch and watch some of the very tall trees in my neighborhood. I like to watch them sway in the wind when a storm is approaching, but I also like to observe them on a calm day when nothing appears to be moving. At the very top of those slender oak trees, though, way up high, some branches are moving slightly. A wind that I can't see on the ground that I can't feel or I can't hear blowing is stirring the leaves. Something is going on in the atmosphere that I'm not aware of as I focus on my work. The wind, though, is still there, influencing the environment and accomplishing nature's purpose.

I still consider myself lucky—or I prefer the word *blessed*—to be a mother, but I also know as a mother, I experience heartache. Yes, there's even been some moaning and wailing on my part, but Jesus' words to the Daughters of Jerusalem say to me, "Take heart, girl, because there's more going on here than what you can see."

FROM MIND TO HEART

What is blessed about being a mother?

What is wretched about being a mother?

What are some examples of green times?

What are some brown or dry times?

When might mourning be misdirected?

When is mourning appropriate?

Are being blessed and being lucky the same thing?

PART II

HE TALKED WITH WHO?!

BUT SHE'S . . .

"I do not condemn you"
(John 8:11).

WHEN MY HUSBAND, BOB, WAS A GRADUATE STUDENT, I WAS A CURRICULUM writer. I didn't make much money, but this work allowed me to stay home with our small children. With Bob's internship, we barely scrimped by. Bob had borrowed an electric typewriter for me to use. (This was in those "ancient days" before word processing.) I could turn out better looking copy and work faster on the electric typewriter rather than with the manual typewriter we owned.

My "office" in our tiny house was located in the utility room right off the kitchen. The utility room wasn't heated, and on a cold winter morning, I wanted to type up something for church, so I decided to move the typewriter into the kitchen where it was warmer. I knew better than to pick up the heavy typewriter and carry it. The stand on which it sat had wheels, so I tried to push the stand into the kitchen. This meant maneuvering a change in floor coverings from linoleum to kitchen carpet. A slightly raised metal ridge separated the two rooms.

When I got to the ridge, the stand balked. I pushed harder. It wouldn't budge. I pushed even harder . . . too hard! The typewriter flew off the stand onto the floor. Oh no, I gasped. You never ever want to drop an electric typewriter. Immediately, shame and remorse washed over me. I felt condemned.

WHAT DOES IT MEAN TO BE CONDEMNED?

• Experiencing strong disapproval from others because of something you said or did. When Bob heard the crash, he came running into the kitchen. He looked at the typewriter in the floor and looked at me as if to say, "What were you thinking? Don't you know better than try to move that heavy typewriter? Why didn't you ask me to help?"

- Having a judgment made against you because of a mistake you made. For example, you made a serious error at work and your boss said, "I'm sorry, we're going to have to let you go." Or you broke a law and were sentenced. "For what you did, you'll be on probation for three years and have to do 100 hours of community service."

- Being declared "unfit," a definition we don't usually apply to people. For example, government officials pronounce a building as no longer usable. Yet if we're honest, we sometimes apply the term *unfit* to people. Your peers might declare you unfit. They close their ranks against you and shut you out from participating in the group because of something you did. Or sadly, you declare yourself unfit. You're convinced that you aren't good for anything.

If you've ever experienced any form of condemnation—and many people have at one time or other—then you will be able to identify with a woman caught committing adultery. You'll understand her embarrassment, her guilt, and her fear as her sin was made public.

HOW IT HAPPENED

Jesus was teaching in Jerusalem during the Festival of Shelters (or Tabernacles) when He was interrupted by some men dragging a disheveled, frightened woman. The commotion surrounding their appearance upped the attention of those who had been listening to Jesus.

The listeners saw the approaching men were Scribes and Pharisees, so they figured their interruption must have something to do with the Law. The Scribes were the teachers and the interpreters of Jewish laws. The Pharisees were members of an influential religious party who were intent on keeping the Law, both the Law of Moses (the written law) and the Traditions of the Elders (the oral law). The Traditions were detailed interpretations and applications of the rules stated in the Law of Moses. Pharisees considered the Traditions as binding as the Law of Moses.

While the Scribes and Pharisees were legal experts, they occasionally took a difficult question to a rabbi, a teacher, to see what he would say. At first the audience assumed this was why the Scribes and Pharisees approached Jesus, but the people soon learned this encounter was about more than a question.

"'Teacher,' they said to Jesus, 'this woman was caught in the very act of committing adultery. In our Law Moses commanded that such a woman must be stoned to death. Now, what do you say?'" (John 8:4-5).

The Scribes and Pharisees didn't really need to ask Jesus about this Law.[1] They understood it. They seemed to have no interest in securing justice or in getting rid of evil, which was the purpose of the Law. If they were truly interested in justice, they would have had the adulterous man brought in too. What was going on? What did the Scribes and the Pharisees really want? They wanted to trap Jesus, and the woman was their bait.

THE TRAP

Over time, the Scribes and Pharisees had become increasingly hostile toward Jesus because of His attitude toward the Traditions of the Elders. Jesus, while respecting and abiding by the Law of Moses, was not into keeping the Traditions. This exasperated the religious leaders, the defenders of the Jewish way of life. As Jesus' popularity with the people increased and His influence spread, their anger grew. They feared Jesus would destroy Judaism as they knew, practiced, and loved. They intended to destroy Him first. This wasn't the first time they had tried, but other efforts had failed.

They felt like they had a sure case against Jesus this time. They would be able to humiliate Jesus and discredit Him in front of the people. But how could a question about interpreting the Law and a woman's guilt be a trap? Here's how.

- *If* Jesus said, "Yes, stone her," two things could happen. (1) Jesus would lose His reputation for mercy; Jesus was a friend of sinners. A yes answer would infuriate the people and separate Jesus from His followers. (2) The Scribes and the Pharisees could report Jesus to the Roman authorities for taking matters into His own hands. Only the Romans, who were in control of the government, could issue the death penalty. Stoning the woman meant killing her.
- *If* Jesus said, "Let her go," He would be accused of not keeping the Law of Moses. It could even be said that Jesus was encouraging people to break the Law of Moses, even encouraging people to commit adultery. To condone the woman's act would obviously and clearly contradict a commandment of God. This would not set well with the people; they would lose their respect for Him.

No matter how Jesus answered, the Scribes and Pharisees were sure their trap was fool proof, but Jesus surprised them. He didn't answer "Yes, stone her" or "Let her go." Instead He didn't answer. Jesus "bent over and wrote on the ground" (John 8:6).

They hadn't expected this reaction! They were confused; nevertheless, they continued pelting Him with questions, and Jesus continued writing. His behavior unnerved them and quieted them which may be why Jesus was writing. If it was the reason, it was working.

As their questioning let up, Jesus stood and looked into their eyes. He said, "Whichever one of you has committed no sin may throw the first stone at her" (v. 7). These legal experts knew what He meant. Jesus was referring to the Mosaic Law where it stated that the witnesses of a crime are "to throw the first stones, and then the rest of the people are to stone that person; in this way you will get rid of this evil" (Deuteronomy 17:7).

Then Jesus "bent over again and wrote on the ground" (John 8:8) again to let the words sink in, and they did. The questioning and the murmuring ceased. No one wanted the personal responsibility of being the one to initiate judgment. No one cast the first stone or the second. One by one, as each took an honest look at himself and faced his own sins, each filed away. The older ones left first, and then the younger ones, until Jesus and the woman were left alone.

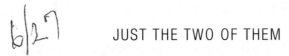

JUST THE TWO OF THEM

As the woman watched them leave, she breathed easier. Stones hadn't been thrown! She was still alive! But it was guarded relief. She hadn't gotten the punishment the Law said she deserved, but would the one man left judge her or have her judged? Would He take her to the Jewish court for an official sentence? Or would He chew her out? Spew out words of harsh condemnation? If He did, what He said wouldn't be any worse than what she was saying to herself. The shame that had washed over her when she was caught was still very much present. She hadn't felt the weight of stones, but she certainly felt the weight of condemnation. What was she going to be fit for now that people knew she had committed adultery? Who would want to associate with her? As she stood there, guilty, yet alive, she expected to hear words of condemnation, but she didn't.

Jesus straightened up from His kneeling position and looked her in the eyes. He said, "'Where are they? Is there no one left to condemn you?" (John 8:10).

"'No one, sir,' she answered" (v. 11).

"'Well, then,' Jesus said, 'I do not condemn you either.'"

Jesus could have said, "You can go now. I'm not going to tell the authorities."

He could have said, "I'm going to have to take you to the Jewish court where they can try you. We need to make the verdict official instead of a vigilante effort because you are guilty."

Or He could have said, "Get out of here now before your accusers come back." If He had, her guilt and condemnation would have remained.

He also could have said, "Don't worry about this. So you were caught. No big deal."

But He said none of these things because she needed to hear the words, "I do not condemn you." If you have ever felt the weight of condemnation, then you can you understand why.

Please say something . . .

Bob never said a word to me about dropping the electric typewriter. I said plenty to myself, though, starting with, *How could I have done such a thing?* And then, *What's Bob going to think of me now? Will this affect his opinion of me?* You might think I was overreacting, but what my husband thinks of me matters. I also considered the ramifications, *How will we pay the owner for this? Where would we get the money to buy a new electric typewriter?* I had gotten myself in this situation, and I couldn't even blame someone else because I was guilty. I had done it, and I was miserable.

All day long I kept waiting for Bob to say something that would make me feel better. There was no angry stare, no glaring at me, nothing in his countenance or posture to indicate he condemned me, but I felt condemned. I needed to hear Bob say, "It's OK" or "I forgive you" or "I don't think any less of you."

Finally around 8:00 that evening I could stand it no longer, I said, "Bob, do you forgive me?"

"For what?"

"For crashing the typewriter?"

Bob said, "Yes, of course. Unforgiveness was never an issue. Now don't worry. We'll work this out some way. I'll start tomorrow by seeing if the typewriter can possibly be fixed."

Ah, I was forgiven! The weight lifted. I needed to know, as the adulterous woman needed to know that she wasn't condemned, and Jesus let her know by speaking the words.

Jesus said, "I do not condemn you" (John 8:11). Could there be any sweeter words to someone who feels the heaviness of condemnation? To someone who has been caught doing something immoral, unlawful, or just plain stupid? To know you're guilty, to be embarrassed or humiliated, to have your sin flaunted among people, to feel all the effects of condemnation, the terror of judgment, and then learn you don't get what you deserve. What a relief! What freedom! And that wasn't all Jesus gave the woman. There was more.

YOU HAVE A FUTURE

Condemnation can stop us in our tracks, make us feel like our life is over. Jesus' words to the adulterous woman indicated that hers wasn't. Besides saying, "I do not condemn you," He also said, "Go, and sin no more" (John 8:11 KJV). In other words, "Don't just stand there. Don't get bogged down by what you've done. Get moving. Your act of adultery does not mean real living has to stop. You've got a future."

Jesus' not condemning her didn't mean He approved of her sin. Neither was He saying that her sin didn't matter or make her wrong behavior any less serious. To continue to sin, though, was not going to do her or anyone else any good. Continuing would thwart her chances for having a meaningful life. If she grabbed hold of her future, wanting to make the most of it, then her future needed to be different than her past. She had a choice: she could go back to her old adulterous ways or she could develop a new way to live. By telling her to "sin no more," Jesus indicated He had confidence in her. He believed she could do better. He was reminding her that obedience pays in the long run.

Just as she had a future, so do we because Jesus wants to say the same thing to us that He said to the adulterous woman. We may be condemned at some time or other in our lives. It may be for some small mistake or misjudgment, or it could be for something major or some where in between.

Regardless of the size, the feeling of heaviness descends. We feel like we've been declared unfit and that nothing will ever go right again.

I don't know about you, but to move beyond condemnation, I need to hear Him say to me what He said to the adulterous woman, "I do not condemn you; go, and sin no more."

You may need to hear Jesus speaking those words through another person; perhaps the one you offended or wronged. Maybe you need to tell a group, admit to something you've been hiding for years. Hearing Him speak through a religious authority—your pastor, a priest, a Bible teacher, or a friend who is dedicated to God may be just what you need.

Sometimes I'm so embarrassed by what I've done that I can only confess it to Jesus. I wouldn't want anyone else to know! To confess, I imagine a conversation with my saying out loud both sides of a dialogue that goes something like this.[2]

BRENDA: *Lord Jesus, are You right here with me?*

JESUS: *Yes, Brenda, I am here with you.*

BRENDA: *Your love for me never changes, does it?*

JESUS: *No, My love for you never changes; I always have and I always will love you.*

BRENDA: *But Lord, how can You? Most of the time I don't even like myself such as right now. I've done something wrong. If I were thinking, I wouldn't have done it, but I did. I'm guilty. I just feel awful, like I'm completely worthless. A feeling of heaviness is weighing me down.*

JESUS: *I understand how you feel, but your insight about yourself, about what you've done, and your future is limited. You can move beyond this because this is not the end of the world. I don't condemn you. You are forgiven. Now go and don't sin anymore. Move forward and embrace the future.*

I realize some readers might question the appropriateness of using imagination like this, but it's one way I can claim this biblical truth: "There is no condemnation now for those who live in union with Christ Jesus" (Romans 8:1). It's a way I can hear Jesus say to me what He said to the adulterous woman, "I do not condemn you" (John 8:11). "Go, and sin no more" (KJV).

FROM MIND TO HEART

6/29

If you had been in the crowd when the Scribes and the Pharisees brought the woman to Jesus, what would you have thought about her? How do you normally react to someone else's moral lapse? Are you judgmental or compassionate?

When Jesus said He didn't condemn the woman, was He saying she wasn't guilty?

Was Jesus saying that the woman's sin didn't matter?

How are we all like this woman?

Do you think she repeated her sin? Or was this the last time she committed adultery?

Is forgiveness of past sins an effective motivator to future moral integrity?

When Jesus said those without guilt should cast the first stone and no person was able to meet His condition, what truth was He revealing about all of us?

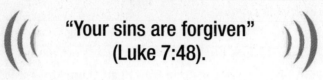

"Your sins are forgiven" (Luke 7:48).

6/30

SOMETIMES WE GET THE IMPRESSION THAT ALL PHARISEES WERE hostile to Jesus, but that's not true, especially early in His Galilean ministry. At this time, His popularity was exploding, which may have been why a Pharisee by the name of Simon invited Jesus to his house for dinner.

Perhaps the idea occurred to Simon when he was in one of the crowds where Jesus was speaking. He thought, *What an unusual person! I'd like to get to know Him.* Or perhaps he had only heard stories about Jesus. After the raising of the Nain widow's son (something we'll talk more about in chap. 12), the "news about Jesus went out through all the country and the surrounding territory" (Luke 7:17).

Regardless of how he heard, Simon's interest was piqued. Who was Jesus? Was He a prophet? Did He have special powers? What did He aim to achieve? Was He going to be a threat to Judaism or be a supporter? To get to know Jesus better—and possibly have his questions answered—Simon did something I would do. He invited Jesus to his house for a meal.

LET THE FEASTING BEGIN

When I want to know people better, I sometimes invite them to my home. Over lunch, dinner, or coffee, conversation flows, and I learn things about the other person. Their words, their gestures, and their manners are insightful. This doesn't mean I watch them intensely!

Rather the natural flow of conversation around the table brings things to light—things that I might not have noticed in another setting.

Simon may have felt the same way. On his home turf, in his familiar space, he could observe Jesus, talk with Him, ask questions, and get to know Him. If Simon invited others, they could compare notes later. This information could be helpful in understanding Jesus, and besides, he could gain some points with his peers. They would be impressed that he hosted a celebrity in his home.

The day of the dinner Simon's house quickly filled with people, both invited guests and uninvited guests. In those days, if a person of renown, particularly a rabbi (teacher) was being hosted, people felt quite free to "drop in" and listen to the celebrity talk.

The invited guests reclined on low couches at tables. Yes, reclined. This is the way they dined. Shoes were off, left at the door when they came in. Feet outstretched behind them. Guests rested on their left elbows leaving the right arm free for eating. The curiosity seekers and the celebrity spotters—the drop-ins—sat around the perimeter of the room.

Simon was pleased with his dinner party. Chatter spiced with laughter filled the room. Everyone seemed to be enjoying themselves, he was getting a chance to check out Jesus, and he was gaining in esteem among his acquaintances. Yes, he would have to say, this was a successful dinner party, and it was until another notorious guest showed up.

7|1 WHAT'S SHE DOING HERE?

In the town where Simon lived was a woman "who lived a sinful life" (Luke 7:37). What does this mean? Doesn't everyone live a sinful life?

Yes, we do. The Bible says "everyone has sinned" (Romans 3:23), but through believing in Jesus we are rescued from the power of sin. Even then we still get off course and sin from time to time. Obviously then, living a sinful life must mean something else. It does.

Living a sinful life, as it is used here, means sinning habitually —having a lifestyle of repeated sin over and over again. This woman was noted for habitual sin. That is, everyone in town knew about her sin, and everyone in the room recognized her. Because she was a woman, because she lived this way, and because everyone knew what she did, the general interpretation has been that she was a prostitute. *The Living Bible* describes her as "a woman of the streets—a prostitute" (Luke 7:37 TLB).

As she crashed the dinner party, Simon thought, *"Oh my, what's* she *doing here? How dare she show up here."*

Fearful what she might do, Simon watched her closely as she moved into the room. He tried to think of a way to get rid of her, but before he could come up with something, she made her way to the guest of honor. She stood "behind Jesus, by his feet" (v. 38).

Simon wondered, *Now what? What does she want? Why did she plant herself at Jesus' feet?* Simon might not understand, but Jesus did. The woman didn't say a word, but she sure communicated with Jesus.

THE BODY SPEAKS

Communication isn't just a matter of words. The way we walk, use our hands, turn our head, wrinkle our forehead, blink our eyes, smile, or move any part of our body communicates. This sinful woman used her body to let Jesus know how she felt about Him, what she needed from Him, and how much faith she had in Him.

Standing behind Jesus, by His feet, the sinful woman began weeping. Her tears fell on His dry, dusty feet, giving them a polka dot effect (clear spots on a gray background). Then her tears became more profuse as she washed His feet with them. "Then she dried his feet with her hair, kissed them, and poured . . . perfume on them" (Luke 7:38).

A Jewish woman didn't let her hair down in public. This was something you just didn't do, but this woman did in order to dry Jesus' feet. She kissed His feet, a true act of humility, and poured perfume on them. The perfume came from an alabaster jar that she carried with her around her neck. Most Jewish women wore this little bottle of costly, concentrated perfume. The sinful woman broke the alabaster jar and poured all the perfume out on Jesus; she held nothing back.

With these actions, the woman spoke. Her gestures and tears said, "I am a sinner. I am repenting. I seek forgiveness. I am showing You my love and adoration. I want to change. I want to be free of sin. I want to be at peace with myself—and peace with God."

To speak in such an emotional way, this woman must have already had some knowledge of Jesus.

- Knowledge that made her realize what He could do for her.
- Knowledge that encouraged her to trust Him to the point of embarrassment and humiliation before a group of men.
- Knowledge that He was trustworthy, totally unlike the other men in her life.
- Knowledge that He was holy, that He was sent from God to help people, and that He had the power to forgive sins.

Where did she learn this? She may have been present when the widow of Nain encountered Jesus. Had she observed His care and consideration for her? Or perhaps "she had listened to Jesus speak from the edge of the crowd, and had glimpsed in Him the hand which would lift her from the mire of her ways."[1] Or maybe it was the stories she had heard about Him. Whenever anyone described something He had done for someone, her heart quickened. *Here's someone,* she concluded, *who can help me if I can just get to Him.* On this day, at Simon's dinner party, she did get to Him, and Jesus forgave her sins without a word actually being said between them.

Simon, though, didn't understand their wordless conversation. When he saw their exchange, he didn't like the impression he was getting. "He said to himself, 'If this man really were a prophet, he would know who this woman is who is touching him; he would know what kind of sinful life she lives!'" (v. 39). At least, he was getting to know Jesus better. He got one of his questions answered so the dinner was serving its purpose.

SIMON'S REACTION

The Pharisee was disgusted at the woman's behavior. Crying and pouring perfume over the guest of honor was completely out of line. He thought Jesus ought to be repulsed by it, but He wasn't. Jesus didn't push the woman away or even frown. Simon didn't say anything out loud, but it didn't matter. Here's another instance of where the body speaks; his face expressed what he was thinking. Jesus noticed "and said to him, 'Simon, I have something to tell you'" (Luke 7:40)

"'Yes, Teacher,' he said, 'tell me.'"

"'There were two men who owed money to a moneylender,' Jesus began. 'One owed him five hundred silver coins, and the other owed him fifty. Neither of them could pay him back, so he canceled the debts of both. Which one, then, will love him more?'" (vv. 41–42).

"'I suppose,' answered Simon, 'that it would be the one who was forgiven more'" (v. 43).

"'You are right,' said Jesus. Then he turned to the woman and said to Simon, 'Do you see this woman? I came into your home, and you gave me no water for my feet, but she has washed my feet with her tears and dried them with her hair. You did not welcome me with a kiss, but she has not stopped kissing my feet since I came. You provided no olive oil for my head, but she has covered my feet with perfume. I tell you, then, the great love she has shown proves that her many sins have been forgiven. But whoever has been forgiven little shows only a little love'" (vv. 43–47).

Jesus' story refers to three things, which were always done when a guest entered a home.

1. The host placed his hand on a guest's shoulder and gave him the kiss of peace — a mark of respect.

2. Water was poured over the guest's feet to clean them and make them feel better, a very kind thing to do because the roads were dusty and shoes were only sandals.

3. Either a pinch of sweet-smelling incense was burned or a drop of rose perfume or ointment was placed on the guest's head.

To do these things was considered good manners, and yet on this occasion, not one of them was done. Simon chose to entertain Jesus to size Him up and to gain esteem, but nothing beyond that. He had not seen this as an opportunity to entertain someone for whom he had high regard. That would have indeed called for good manners.

Simon had the same opportunity to seek forgiveness as the woman, but he didn't. Jesus' story and concluding line showed that Simon didn't feel the need. As a Pharisee, he felt he was a good man in the sight of others and of God. No forgiveness was needed. The woman, on the other hand, was very conscious of her sinful life, sought forgiveness, and was overwhelmed with love for Jesus.

Jesus' story was for Simon, but He "turned to the woman" as He talked (v. 44). She heard what Jesus said, and she must have been deeply touched by Jesus' defense of her tears and gift of perfume. Jesus said to Simon "the great love she has *shown* proves that her many sins have been forgiven" (v. 47; author's italics). Following this conclusion, Jesus turned to her and said, "Your sins are forgiven" (v. 48).

If there was even a smattering of lingering doubt, even a little speck that didn't get communicated through body language, it was taken care of with these reaffirming words.

The woman doesn't appear to be surprised by Jesus' words. It's as if she was certain that if she could just get to Him, then she would experience forgiveness. The guests, however, were flabbergasted.

THE BAFFLED GUESTS

While Jesus said to her, "Your sins are forgiven" (Luke 7:48), the guests sat up and took notice. They "began to say to themselves, 'Who is this, who even forgives sins?'" (v. 49).

The pace of the dinner chatter picked up. "This man is very unusual. He has done things that we've known no other man to do, but forgive sin?"

"Come on! Who does He think He is?"

"Everyone knows only God can forgive sin. Yet here is Jesus pronouncing forgiveness and not to just anyone. He's saying this to a notorious sinner!"

"Can her habitual sin really be forgiven?"

"Isn't Jesus taking on God's role by saying she's forgiven? Isn't this blasphemy?"

Talk about revealing dinner conversations! Jesus' nature was certainly unveiling itself. Simon's guests were getting to know Jesus better, even if they didn't like what they were learning. Some of Simon's questions were being answered, and some new questions were being asked.

Jesus could hear the men's animated conversation—if not the words, then the tone—but He didn't try to defend His position, His actions, or His words. The time would come when people would realize He was God and that faith in Him could save a person from her sins. It was the woman's faith that had saved her (see verse 50).

The woman's action—her finding Jesus, entering a dinner party uninvited, expressing her emotions freely, and being confident He would respond exemplified stellar faith.

- He did not forgive her because of her love, although she did love Him.
- He did not forgive her because someone ought to help a woman like this.
- He did not forgive her because she could express her emotions well.
- He did not forgive her because she expressed herself in a loving and emotional way.
- He did not forgive her because she was sinned against.
- He forgave her because she had faith.

Now she had something precious, more precious than an alabaster jar, to carry with her as she reentered life in the village. Jesus said, "Go in peace" (v. 50), and she did because she was forgiven.

7/5   SURPRISED OR NOT SURPRISED?

The sinful woman didn't appear to be surprised by Jesus' words, "Your sins are forgiven," but the dinner guests were. What about you? Were you surprised or not surprised by what He said?

If you identified with this woman and her lifestyle of sin, then you might be awed by the possibility of being forgiven so much. This isn't insinuating that you are a prostitute! A habitual lifestyle of sin may take on many forms. As you wrestle with your sin, its fallout in your life, its deception, and the peace-disturbing guilt that accompanies the sin, you might have concluded your situation was hopeless. There's no way you could be saved, but Jesus' words to this sinful woman can say to you, too, that forgiveness is possible!

Or perhaps you were surprised if you believe that goodness secures God's favor. This belief may be a part of your faith tradition, or it could be a belief you picked up from others. In conversations, for example, people often express hope that they are good enough to get into heaven. Jesus' words to this woman indicate that it is faith in Him and not good behavior that counts.

On the other hand, maybe you weren't moved at all by this woman's experience and the words Jesus said to her. This is the way Jesus should act! All a person needs to do is say the sinner's prayer or walk the aisle of a church and tell the pastor you want to be saved, and you are saved. Nothing to it. Where's the marvel? The years have passed and a lot of living got in the way and you lost the wonder of having your sins forgiven.

Maybe you need your wonder renewed. One way to do this is to go back in memory to the time when you were seeking forgiveness. What happened? Why did you need Jesus? What was your life like at the time? What did He say to you? What were you like afterward? Better yet, tell someone the story of your conversion. Giving our testimonies breathes new life in us, bringing back the wonder of being forgiven.

Nowhere to give your testimony? Invite someone to dinner. Conversation over food is a great opportunity to renew wonder and give a witness at the same time. Be careful. When your guest leaves and you start the clean up, you just might find yourself singing, "How marvelous! how wonderful! Is my Saviour's love for me!"[2]

FROM MIND TO HEART

Have you ever felt the way this woman did? Because of your sin, have you wanted to touch Him and to anoint Him?

What do you think was going through the woman's head as she listened to Simon and Jesus talk?

What did it mean to her to have her sins forgiven?

Jesus called her a woman of faith. How was this sinful woman a person of faith?

How does this woman's faith compare with that of the Syrophoenician woman's faith?

What did those who heard Jesus tell the woman her sins were forgiven say among themselves? When might we be tempted to say something similar?

PART III

HE'S WHAT?

CHAPTER 9

"I am . . . living water"
(John 4:10 TLB).

ONCE WHEN I WAS SPEAKING IN ST. LOUIS, THE PROGRAM LISTED ME as living in my hometown of Ramsey, Illinois, rather than where I live. My speaking that day went well. Women came up to me afterward and told me how much they appreciated the talk. Some of them were from a town near Ramsey. In fact, our small towns were basketball rivals. As they lingered, they kept saying, "I can't believe you are from Ramsey." In other words, how could someone from *Ramsey* of all places be a convention speaker and give a quality speech?

When I lived in Chicago, a certain ethnic group was continually the butt of jokes. When I was in graduate school in Texas, one Texan said to me, "I can't believe I'm friends with a *Yankee*." One state I lived in had put-down jokes about everyone in the state below us. (I imagine that state had jokes about the state above them too.) Isn't it amazing how we categorize places and people?

This kind of thing occurs around the world with some characterizations being very deep and hateful, and it appears in the Bible as well. One particular clash between two groups forms the backdrop for the longest recorded conversation Jesus had with a woman.

OH, THOSE SAMARITANS!

The little region of Palestine, where Jesus lived and traveled, had several political regions, including Samaria. The Samaritans were scorned by the residents of the other regions even though they historically had been one people, the Israelites. Under Moses's

91

leadership, they covenanted with God to be His people and follow His laws.

Later, in the days of King David and King Solomon, the Israelites were united, but after Solomon died, they split into two kingdoms: Israel (the Northern Kingdom of which Samaria was the capital) and Judah (the Southern Kingdom with Jerusalem as its capital).

The Israelites of the Northern Kingdom had no sustained interest in being God's people. Although they claimed to still believe in Him, they were continually tempted by idolatry and consequently grew weak. The powerful Assyrians conquered and dispersed many of them to the far corners of their empire. The Assyrians sent citizens from other defeated nations to live among the Israelites, who blended their identities, beliefs, and practices with those of the other nations. These Israelites were far from being a distinctive people as God intended them to be. They even built their own place of worship on Mt. Gerizim rather than worship at the Temple Solomon had built in Jerusalem.

Around 586 BC, the people of Judah were conquered by the Babylonians, and the Temple in Jerusalem destroyed. The people were taken captive, but eventually they were allowed to return home where they started rebuilding the Temple. When the Israelites (called Jews) rejected their northern neighbors' (the Samaritans) offer to help rebuild, the groups became bitter enemies.

In 108 BC, some Jews from Judah (which became Judea) destroyed the Samaritan temple on Mt. Gerizim, while the Jerusalem temple remained intact. This increased the hostility, which continued to intensify so that by Jesus' time, Jews avoided contact with the Samaritans. They even took inconvenient travel routes to avoid contact with them. Not Jesus, though—He took the direct route.

When a crisis developed in Judea where He was preaching, He decided to go to Galilee. He took the Samaritan route instead of crossing the Jordan River and traveling through Perea to circumnavigate Samaria. Jesus refused to be defined or limited by man-made divisions. All people were valued and respected in His eyes. In who He was, He could not do otherwise. He "had to go through Samaria" (v. 4 NIV).

Traveling through Samaria, Jesus and His disciples came to a town called Sychar, about 40 miles from Jerusalem in Judea. This area was special to the Samaritans because Jacob had given this land to his son Joseph. Located at the foot of Mount Gerizim, this is where the Samaritans had built their temple, the one their neighbors to the south, the Jews of Judea, had destroyed.

Jacob's well was located outside Sychar. Jesus was tired from the journey by the time they arrived. He sat down to rest, and the disciples went off to buy food.

"It was about noon" (John 4:6 NIV). This would make it a good time to rest because He would be alone. People came earlier in the day or later in the day to draw water when it wasn't so hot. His rest, however, was interrupted when a Samaritan woman arrived at the well.

This woman wasn't seeking Jesus or looking for a spiritual experience. She was there to get water. She didn't ask Jesus for anything or even speak to Him. He could have continued meditating without interruption, but that's not what He did. He initiated a conversation with her. He didn't start with "Hello" or "Good morning" or "Nice day today, isn't it?" Instead He surprised her with a request. Jesus said, "Give me a drink of water" (v. 7).

YOU WANT WHAT FROM ME?!?

Much aware of how Jews felt toward Samaritans, she knew they refused to eat or drink from a vessel used by a Samaritan. If they did, Jews would be considered religiously unclean. Neither did good Jewish men talk with Samaritan women, and yet here was a Jewish man speaking to her. She was perplexed. "You are a Jew and I am a Samaritan woman. How can you ask me for a drink?" (John 4:9 NIV).

Jesus didn't offer any explanation. He didn't say, "I don't recognize man-made barriers. I'm not into categorizing people." Instead He made another puzzling statement. He said to her, "If you knew the gift of God and who it is that asks you for a drink, you would have asked him and he would have given you living water" (v. 10 NIV).

At this point, she must have thought, *This man is strange! He's Jewish and I'm a Samaritan, and He asks me for a drink, and now He's talking about a gift from God and living water. There's just well water here; there's no living water.*

Water was available in plentiful supply only during the rainy season of the year. During that time, the people collected water in cisterns (wells) so that when the rainy season ended, they would still have water. Collected water was what was available at Jacob's well.

Living water, on the other hand, meant running water or flowing water. If you got living water in this Palestinian area, a person would have to delve down really deep, and yet this man said He could give her living water. How could He do that? Even if He could dig deep enough to reach living water, He had no bucket. He had no container of any kind to retrieve the water. *What's He thinking? He must be out of touch with reality, or I'm missing something here.*

With a touch of sarcasm she said to Jesus, "Where can you get this living water? Are you greater than our father Jacob, who gave us the well and drank from it himself, as did also his sons and his livestock?" (vv. 11–12 NIV). She didn't think so!

What the woman didn't realize was that Jesus was introducing a metaphor to teach her about a quality of life that could be hers. Jesus was a master at using metaphors to help His listeners understand themselves and their need for God. On other occasions He described Himself as bread, as a vine, as a door, and as a shepherd. In this way, He used something people readily connect to in order to grasp spiritual truths.

Jesus used the metaphor of living water to help her—and us—grasp what He can give her. To fully appreciate the significance of this metaphor, we need to go back to "before Jacob," back to Creation.

When God created humans, He created us in His image.[1] We don't know all that means, but we do know it means we are built with a longing for Him. God designed us this way so we would be drawn to Him. This inner longing may be described as a spiritual thirst, one that living water will satisfy. You will know you have swallowed this living water if you feel connected with God, if your life has meaning and purpose, and if you feel the presence of the Holy Spirit in your life.

IT'S YOURS FOR THE ASKING

As Jesus said to the Samaritan woman, we can ask "him and he" will give us "living water" (John 4:10 NIV). This may take the form of a simple, sincere prayer that recognizes your belief in Him. "Jesus, I've heard about Your Living Water. I'm thirsty, and I want to drink this water. I want a relationship with You."

Or the prayer could be more intense and complicated depending on our circumstances. We may need to agonize before the Lord, particularly if we have tried to satisfy our spiritual thirst in some other way.

- Drinking of the fountain of fame.
- Taking huge gulps from the well of worldly pleasure.
- Swallowing big amounts from the lake of earthly learning.
- Slurping continuously from the sea of success.
- Sipping from the fountain of drugs or alcohol until that's all we want to do.
- Lapping up water from the fountain of human relationships, scarching for affection that will satisfy out inner thirst.

Someday, we believe, if we keep drinking at one of these fountains, our compelling thirst will be satisfied. Truthfully some satisfaction may occur initially, but it will not last. We'll keep drinking and drinking and wonder why our thirst is never quenched. That's because God created our thirst, and He also gave us the thirst quencher. Jesus is "the gift of God." Yes, the One who gives us Living Water is also the gift of God. When you receive the gift, something else becomes possible.

A SPRING OF WATER WELLING UP

In continuing His thought-provoking conversation, Jesus pointed to Jacob's well and said to the woman, "Everyone who drinks this water will be thirsty again, but whoever drinks the water I give them will never thirst. Indeed, the water I give them will become in them a spring of water welling up to eternal life" (John 4:13–14 NIV).

The water Jesus gives truly satisfies a person's spiritual thirst as He takes up residence in our inner space, but there's more! This water becomes a well or a spring within a person. No stagnant water here! Rather it leaps with power as the Holy Spirit works in our lives.[2] Bible versions describe it this way.

- "A spring of water welling up to eternal life" (NIV).
- "A spring which will provide . . . life-giving water" (GNT).
- "A well of water springing up to eternal life" (NASB).
- "A spring of water that keeps on bubbling up" (4:14 Williams).

My personal favorite is the last description because that's how I think of the Holy Spirit working—bubbling up, reassuring me that He is present, real, and active. I think that's how one of my fellow Christian writers feels too. In one of her blogs, after her book on fear came out, Christin Ditchfield admitted that while she conquers some fears in her life, she still has all kinds of other stresses, pressures, drama, and trauma. She wrote, "My life is full of it. It's part of the human condition. But beneath it all, I find this undercurrent, this stream that's bubbling up into a noisy, gurgling, irrepressible joyful spring."[3]

R. A. Torrey put it this way: "It is a great thing to have a well that we can carry with us; to have a well that is within us; to have our source of satisfaction not in the things outside ourselves, but in the well within that is always springing up in freshness and power."[4] This well of "life-giving water" is with us through out this life and beyond. Sounds incredible, doesn't it? It did to the Samaritan woman, too, only in a different way.

7/10 "GIVE ME THAT WATER!"

The woman's eyes lit up as she heard the advantages of having living water. "'Sir,' the woman said, 'give me that water! Then I will never be thirsty again, nor will I have to come here to draw water'" (John 4:15).

Having this water would save her time! If she wasn't ever thirsty, she wouldn't have to come to the well every day to draw water. If that was what Jesus was offering, then she wanted Living Water! It would make her life easier.

The Samaritan woman still didn't get what Living Water was. She only saw what was right before her eyes and how advantageous Living Water would be to her work load. She didn't catch the spiritual meaning behind the Living Water metaphor. Instead, she thought of the work she had to do.

On the other hand, maybe she was beginning to understand, and she was a tad uncomfortable with what she heard. Her linking Living Water with reality might have been a decoy to keep from dealing with what Jesus was really saying. If she caught on to the spiritual meaning of Living Water, she might have to do some inner cleaning. If there's going to be room for the "gift of God," then space must be made for the gift.

For her and for us, this means getting rid of sin. Sin fans out and fills up our inner space, where that inner longing for God exists. Sin is deceptive by nature; it makes us think it's not really there. We take offense if someone so much as suggests we are sinners. And yet if we want to drink Living Water, if we want a well of Living Water bubbling up within us, we must clean our inner space by confessing our sin and recognizing our need for God. Jesus wanted to help the Samaritan woman do this so He called her attention to where she was in life.

"'Go and call your husband,' Jesus told her, 'and come back'" (v. 16).

Whoa, she hadn't seen this coming! Now she really felt uncomfortable! She didn't like feeling this way, but she swallowed hard, and replied, "I don't have a husband" (v. 17).

"Jesus replied, 'You are right when you say you don't have a husband. You have been married to five men, and the man you live with now is not really your husband. You have told me the truth'" (vv. 17–18).

The woman recoiled at being so exposed. She immediately went into a self-defense mode by bringing up differences between Jews and Samaritans.

CHANGING THE SUBJECT

"'I see you are a prophet, sir,' the woman said" (John 4:19). The Jews believed in prophets, but not the Samaritans. They only accepted the Pentateuch (the first five books of the Bible), but if there were such a thing as a prophet, then perhaps Jesus was one. After all, He could certainly see things others couldn't see!

Then she brought up their different places of worship. She said, "My Samaritan ancestors worshiped God on this mountain, but you Jews say that Jerusalem is the place where we should worship God" (v. 20).

In other words, she was trying to distract Him by getting Jesus to debate about the best place to worship. It was her way of saying, "Let's not talk about me. Let's get into differences between Jews and Samaritans."

But the truth is we have to "talk" if we want Living Water. We have to acknowledge who we are and what's filling up our inner space. We have to clear it out through confession and repentance so there will be room for Living Water and the well that springs up into eternal life. We have to ask the Giver for the Gift of God. This kind of "talk" is something we all need to keep in mind—and practice—even if we have received the Living Water.

WHEN THE BUBBLING STOPS

If you have a decorative fountain in your yard, you know that it requires some diligence on your part to keep it working. Leaves can't be allowed to gather and pile up. Dirt must be cleaned out from time to time. Trash might need to be cleared after a wind storm has blown through. But all of this work is worth it because of the enjoyment the fountain brings.

In a similar way, the *well* of Living Water in us can become blocked by some worldly conformity, some act of disobedience, or even weariness in well doing. I know because it happened to me when I was living in Chicago.

I became a Christian (asked for and received the Living Water) when growing up in Ramsey, Illinois. From that point on, I earnestly tried to please God. This doesn't mean I always succeeded, but it does mean I exerted a lot of effort. By the time my college years were coming to an end, I had grown weary of trying to make all my decisions in terms of what God wanted. I slowly closed myself off from listening to His voice. I took a job in a Chicago suburb without even asking for God's leadership. Outwardly nothing changed, but inwardly something had. The well of Living Water was blocked; it didn't bubble up any longer. The Living Water was still there—I was still a Christian, but the effervescent joy was gone.

I mulled over losing this joy for months before I unblocked the fountain and it could spring into action once again. I put it off because repentance and confession can be painful. I did this, though, because I wanted the Holy Spirit to work in my life again.

I tell this about myself because I've seen this same kind of desire in the eyes of women singing, "Fill my cup, Lord" or quoting Psalm 42:1: "As a deer longs for a stream of cool water, so I long for you, O God." I want these women to know their thirst can be satisfied. The well of Living Water can bubble up in their souls if they will "talk" with Jesus. I know He wants to talk with them.

It took more conversation—even more than a metaphor—for the Samaritan woman to open herself to Jesus, as we'll see in the next chapter. Nevertheless, this part of her conversation helps us understand our spiritual thirst, how it can truly be satisfied, and how it can bring joy into our lives here on earth and on into eternity.

FROM MIND TO HEART

What does this conversation have in common with the conversations Jesus had with the adulterous woman (chap. 7) and the prostitute (chap. 8) at Simon's dinner party?

What need does Living Water fill?

Who do we ask for Living Water?

What or who is "the Gift of God"?

What might prevent a person from receiving "the Gift of God"?

What might keep the spring of Living Water from welling up within a person?

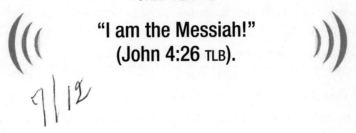

CHAPTER 10

"I am the Messiah!"
(John 4:26 TLB).

FOCUSING ON THE SURPRISE ELEMENT IN JESUS' CONVERSATIONS WITH women doesn't mean there's always one. As we grow closer in our relationship with Jesus, we may know what to expect in some instances. We count on Him in the way we do with a good friend, "I knew you were going to say that." But there's also the possibility that we will be spiritually surprised. He may say something totally unexpected. This was the way it was with the Samaritan woman. In fact, she received a surprise within a surprise.

THE SURPRISE

At Jacob's Well near Sychar, Jesus asked this woman for a drink of water. As we saw in the last chapter, she responded with, "You are a Jew and I am a Samaritan woman. How can you ask me for a drink?" (John 4:9 NIV).

She was surprised that Jesus would talk with her because she had three strikes against her.

1. She was a Samaritan and Jews did "not associate with Samaritans" (John 4:9 NIV).

2. She was a woman. Rabbinic documents warned Jewish men against speaking to a woman in public.

3. She was a sinner. People snubbed her and talked about her because of her lifestyle. She lived with a man who was not her husband after having multiple husbands. That's why she was at the well at midday when other people weren't there. She could avoid the stares and whispers of others.

Jesus, though, talked with her! His request for a drink wasn't to satisfy His thirst; it was a conversation starter. The talk that followed was interesting and stimulating until Jesus got too personal. When Jesus revealed that He knew all about her, she changed the subject. She brought up a much-discussed and sometimes contentious topic about the right place to worship, the kind of topic that can still come up today.

MY PLACE IS BETTER THAN YOUR PLACE

The Samaritan woman pointed out that her ancestors worshiped God on Mount Gerizim, right in the area where they were talking. She added, "But you Jews claim that the place where we must worship is in Jerusalem" (John 4:20 NIV).

The Jews worshiped at the Temple on Mount Zion in Jerusalem in Judea and claimed it was a holy place. The Jerusalem Temple was built before the Samaritans built a temple on Mount Gerizim. They rewrote Scripture and tampered with history to justify and to glorify their position. This greatly irked the Jews. In the late second century BC, they destroyed the Mount Gerizim temple. You can imagine how that fueled the hostility between Jews and Samaritans.

Now as Jesus and the woman talked, only the ruins of a temple once located in her area remained; nevertheless, the Samaritans still held Mount Gerizim as sacred. They argued with the Jews that it was *the* place to worship. It's hard to let go of our "spots."

In a recent conversation, a woman told me she went to church "in town," meaning the small town where she lived. She continued, "Our church is very small; less than 25 people attend. I wish for something larger so that my little daughter could benefit more. There's a church 'out in the country' that's with our denomination. This church is also small, running less than 25. I wish the two churches would combine so we could offer more and have a fuller experience."

I asked, "Well, can't you?"

She said, "No, we can't. The townspeople won't go out in the country to church, and the country people won't come to town!"

This isn't the only incident I've heard like this. Like Jews and Samaritans, many want to hold on to what they've had, feeling their place of worship is the best place to worship and sometimes like it's the only place.

The Samaritan woman's motive, though, wasn't about preserving a spot. She brought up the different worship places to change the subject, to get the spotlight off of her. Her ploy didn't work. Jesus didn't debate the issue as she had hoped. Instead He taught her about true worship.

WORSHIP IS ABOUT MORE THAN PLACE

The Living Water metaphor Jesus used to turn the woman's thoughts to spiritual matters was put aside; it was time to be direct and emphatic. Jesus began, "Woman . . . believe me" (John 4:21 NIV). In other words, "I'm going to say something—something important—and I want you to listen up and take in what I'm saying."

He continued, "A time is coming when you will worship the Father neither on this mountain nor in Jerusalem. You Samaritans worship what you do not know; we worship what we do know, for salvation is from the Jews. Yet a time is coming and has now come when the true worshipers will worship the Father in spirit and in truth, for they are the kind of worshipers the Father seeks. God is spirit, and his worshipers must worship in the Spirit and in truth'" (vv. 21–24 NIV).

A time was coming when Jews and Samaritans would not need a

particular mountain or a certain temple to find God. Men and women would be able to find God everywhere. Those who truly sought God would find God in every place.

This is not to say some places aren't more conducive to worship than others are. Our surroundings can affect the quality of our worship, but confining God to a particular place as in, "This is the *only* place where God can be worshiped" or "Where I worship is a better than where you worship" is wrong. True worshippers grasp the largeness of God. They know He can be worshipped in a magnificent temple, in a cabin in the woods, in a crowded church, in one where few people are present, in a car on the way to work, while doing mundane chores, or any of a number of places. God is not confined to certain *places* because "God is spirit" (v. 24 NIV). Recognizing this enables people to "worship in the Spirit and in truth."

True worship is when our spirit speaks to and meets with God and He responds to us. Both Jews and Samaritans needed to believe this so the difference between which mountain was holy was not worth arguing about. Jesus did, though, make a statement about Jews that could make Samaritans bristle and fight back. He said, "You Samaritans worship what you do not know; we worship what we do know, for salvation is from the Jews" (v. 22 NIV).

FIGHTING WORDS

If Jesus were debating, then saying, "We know what you don't know" sounds arrogant and snobbish. Such words make you want to defend your group, but Jesus wasn't debating. He was teaching. With these words, Jesus let the Samaritan woman know that all along God's plan for redemption was through His people who came to be known as Jews. The Samaritans had once been a part of this family before they went their separate way.

God's plan was to anoint someone out of the tribe of Judah. *Anointing* is often mentioned in the Old Testament. Most frequently the word was used in connection with kings, priests, and prophets. In all of these instances, these people were anointed ones, but the Messiah—the One who was to come—would be the Anointed One. The word *Messiah* comes from the Hebrew verb *mashach*, which means "to anoint," and therefore the Messiah is "Anointed One." In the Greek, "Christ" means the Anointed One. He would be a Suffering Servant who would save men and women from their sins.

The prophetic books indicated the Messiah's Jewish lineage. The Samaritans, though, didn't read or recognize these books, so the woman may not have heard anything about salvation coming from the Jews. This didn't mean only Jews could be saved. Salvation would be for all, including Samaritans. The one, though, who would make this possible would be a Jew.

How quickly the woman was catching on to what Jesus was teaching is hard to say. Even if she were "getting it," she may have been confused by Jesus' saying, "A *time is coming* and *has now come* when the true worshipers will worship the Father in the Spirit and in truth" (John 4:23 NIV; author's italics). This is confusing. How could a time be both coming and now has come?

This is possible because a process was involved. Jesus, the One who would make it possible for all of us to understand true worship, was right there with her as He was with others. In the flesh, He was ministering and teaching, letting people know what God was like. In that sense, the time "has now come." The process, though, still needed to be completed, and it would be with Jesus' death on the Cross, His resurrection, and the outpouring of His Spirit. In that way, a time was coming.

At Pentecost, when the Holy Spirit would be manifested, Jesus would be available to all believers and not just a select few. Once that happened, men and women, and boys and girls everywhere would be able to worship Him in spirit and in truth, the way that pleases God.

As Jesus taught the Samaritan woman about true worship, God's redemptive plan, and about God's nature, there was no suggestion on His part that theology was something He couldn't discuss with her. Neither was He offended nor upset by the questions she raised. She didn't have to remain silent in His presence, and she didn't. The disciples were reluctant to ask Jesus questions (see John 4:27), but she wasn't! Asking question is a good way to learn, and did she ever learn!

THE SURPRISE WITHIN A SURPRISE

The woman who had planned to ignore the lone Jewish male at the well instead became involved in a stimulating conversation. Seldom had any male treated her with such respect. Jesus listened to her every word. She was touched by this, yet bewildered.

Through their conversation about Living Water, about her life, and about God's being Spirit, the woman sensed something significant happening. This was not the usual talk people had at the well where pleasantries about the weather were exchanged. This man's words were so different; He was so knowledgeable. She wondered, *Who is He? Where did He come from?*

"You know, He has to be someone special," she said to herself. "He's so different from anyone I have ever talked with, and my spirit stirs within me when He talks. I feel both rumblings of discontent and feelings of excitement, as if I'm on the threshold of learning something big."

As she processed all this, an idea occurred to her. It wasn't anything she was really sure about; it was just a possibility. Could He be the Messiah? Even though she wouldn't have been taught that salvation was from the Jews, she was taught to expect a Messiah. Both Jews and Samaritans were looking for one, but their expectations were different.

The Jews, for the most part, expected the Messiah to be a political, military type of person—a deliverer. They were looking for—and longing for—a human king on the order of King David. They expected God to send a "Son of David" who would destroy their enemies. The messianic kingdom He set up would be an earthly kingdom with Jerusalem as its capital.

The Samaritans, on the other hand, expected a teacher-lawgiver messiah. They were anticipating someone like Moses because he had said, "The LORD your God will raise up for you a prophet like me from among you" (Deuteronomy 18:15 NIV). This prophet would have God's "words in his mouth" and "He will tell [people] everything" (v. 18 NIV).

Growing up in Samaria, this Moses-type of messiah is what the woman would have been taught to expect, and this man before her was certainly teaching her! He taught her about spiritual thirst and how it could be satisfied. He taught her about herself and about true worship. As she went over these things, her thoughts picked up speed and galloped toward a conclusion: *He's the Messiah*. As if to test this possibility, this woman who had kept pace with Jesus in every part of their conversation said out loud, "I know that the Messiah will come, and when he comes, he will tell us everything" (John 4:25).

Jesus, who never used the term *Messiah* with reference to Himself in public address, said to this woman of Samaria, "I am the Messiah!" (v. 26 TLB).

She must have thought, *Wow! I can't believe this is happening to me. I just came to the well to get water, and here I am, meeting the Messiah.*

If she said anything is unlikely because the disciples returned from buying food in Sychar. With their arrival, she immediately felt the curtain of cultural disapproval descend. The disciples didn't actually say anything to her, but she could read their thoughts. She knew they were shocked to find Jesus talking with a woman. Their disapproval, though, didn't take anything away from what she had experienced and the exuberance she felt. She had to tell someone or she would burst.

I HAVE TO TELL SOMEONE

Her experience was so phenomenal she hurried back to Sychar, even leaving her water jar behind in the urgency of the moment. She didn't stop to consider the attitude of the townspeople toward her or wonder if they would listen to her. She had news that couldn't be kept! Even though she was out of breath by the time she arrived, she still managed to blurt out, "Come and meet a man who told me everything I ever did! Can this be the Messiah?" (John 4:28–29 TLB).

Literally, her question was, "This man could not be the Messiah, could He?" It was her way of saying, "I had an unbelievable experience today! Someone we've been looking for arrived here in Samaria. It started out to be just an ordinary day, but it turned into an extraordinary one when He talked with me. He read me like a book. How could someone we've been looking for and waiting for appear to someone like me? How could He know so much about me? Is there any other explanation besides His being the Messiah? If there is, please tell me!"

I imagine there were those who wanted to say, "You're nuts," because they had little regard for her and her story was so outrageous. Nevertheless, her excitement was so strong they couldn't resist being interested. "Everything? Someone told you everything? A possible Messiah right here in Sychar?"

Her story was too unusual, too out of the ordinary. They had to see for themselves, and they did. They went to Jesus, and they learned He was the Messiah. He taught them for two days as He had taught the Samaritan woman. At first their interest was "because of the woman's testimony, 'He told me everything I ever did'" (v. 39 NIV). But after Jesus taught them, they became believers "because of his words" (v. 41 NIV).

The new believers "said to the woman, 'We no longer believe just because of what you said; now we have heard for ourselves, and we know that this man really is the Savior of the world'" (v. 42 NIV).

And isn't this what we want? I do! I want that pulsating, throbbing conviction inside me that says Jesus really is the Messiah. He really was—and is—the One sent from God to be "the Savior of the world." I want this conviction not because a Samaritan woman learned He was the Messiah or because some Sychar residents believed, but because I meet Him and learn from Him. I want the Teacher to teach me, and He does through His Spirit (see verse 26 NIV). This is why having conversations with Jesus is so important. We are in the learner's seat where we can listen to the Teacher, and who knows? A surprise element may be involved—maybe even a surprise within a surprise—that keeps alive the sense of knowing in our hearts—a knowing which leads us to worship Him in spirit and in truth.

FROM MIND TO HEART

How can a woman today "take heart" from Jesus' conversation with the Samaritan woman?

Why do you think Jesus admitted He was the Messiah in a private conversation with a woman rather than admitting it in front of a large crowd?

What did Jesus' being the Messiah mean to the Samaritans and to her in particular? What does it mean to us? Does it matter that He was — and is — the Messiah?

What does it mean to worship God in spirit and in truth?

What kind of worshippers does God seek?

If the disciples hadn't returned with food when they did, what do you think the Samaritan woman might have said when Jesus admitted to being the Messiah?

When have you been moved to say to others, "Come, see a man"? When have you been so excited about Jesus that you left something behind or undone to tell others?

The Samaritans said why they believed Jesus was the Messiah. Why do you believe?

7/16

CHAPTER 11

))) "I am the resurrection and the life" (John 11:25 NIV). (((

WHEN WE EXPERIENCE A CRISIS, WE EXPECT OUR CLOSE FRIENDS TO "be there" for us. This expectation is so ingrained that we assume they will show up. We don't even have to ask.

Martha, whom we looked at in chapter 3, and her siblings, Mary and Lazarus, were friends with Jesus. He loved them[1] and they loved Him, so when Mary and Martha faced a crisis, they assumed they could count on Jesus. He would "show up" when they needed Him. Instead Jesus surprised them. He didn't appear when they thought He should.

WHERE WAS JESUS?

After visiting Martha, Mary, and Lazarus in Bethany in Judea,[2] Jesus went on to nearby Jerusalem. After that He and His disciples moved into the countryside of Judea. They wanted to avoid the increasing hostility of the Jews in Jerusalem.

The tension, though, followed Him into the Judean countryside, so Jesus and His disciples moved on to Perea. The Pereans were more open-minded and less critical than the Judeans so Jesus and His team could minister freely.

While in Perea, a messenger from the Bethany sisters arrived. He said to Jesus, "Lord, the one you love is sick" (John 11:3 NIV). That's what he said, but the implied message was, "Please do something."

While the women hadn't spelled out specifically what they wanted, they believed Jesus could and would help them. Martha,

110

Mary, and Lazarus had heard stories about how Jesus healed people and exorcised demons; maybe they had even witnessed some of His miracles. Whether they had or hadn't, they were conscious of His power and knew He was their friend. The sisters believed Jesus would help them. In their way of thinking, just knowing Lazarus was gravely ill should prompt Jesus to stop what He was doing and return to Bethany.[3] Instead He stayed where He was two whole days before returning. When He arrived, Lazarus had been dead four days.

In the meantime, Martha and Mary contended with their sadness at losing Lazarus, the arranging of his burial, and the hosting of the mourners who came to grieve with them. All of this dominated their attention, and yet they questioned Jesus' absence. Where was He? Why didn't He come? They were confused and hurt because they had been so sure He would. After all, friends help friends.

Lazarus was buried shortly after he died. Immediate burial was essential because Jews did not prepare their dead carefully by embalming. Families wrapped the deceased in grave cloths and quickly buried the body, and then the mourning began. Friends assisted in this grief work, although sometimes professional mourners were used. The mourning included tearing garments, wailing loudly, and playing flutes. The mourners usually sat on the floor and cried loudly to the accompaniment of the flutes. Amidst this noise, Martha somehow heard someone say that Jesus was coming. She left the mourners and Mary behind and headed out to meet Him. Maybe now she would get some answers.

ANSWERS AND MORE

The first thing she said when she saw Jesus was, "If you had been here, Lord, my brother would not have died!" (John 11:21). Martha voiced what Mary (v. 32) and some of the mourners (v. 37) were also thinking.

As soon as she said, "If you had been here," she realized how harsh the words sounded, and she softened her tone. Seeing Jesus face-to-face reminded her of the confidence she had in Him. She said, "But I know that even now God will give you whatever you ask him for" (v. 22). Besides, a small part of her still hoped that Jesus might act on their behalf and make things better. Her hope was not disappointed.

Jesus said to Martha, "Your brother will rise again" (John 11:23 NIV).

What? How's that again? The furrows in Martha's forehead deepened as she tried to understand what Jesus said. *How could her brother rise again? He was in a tomb!* Some of those stories her family had heard were about Galilean miracles where Jesus brought people back to life. He had raised the son of the widow of Nain (Luke 7:11–17) and the daughter of Jairus (Mark 5:21–43), but in each of these incidents the person had just died. Lazarus had been dead four days! His body had started to decompose. She had never heard of someone being dead as long as Lazarus and being brought back to life. *Surely*, she thought, *Jesus must be speaking of life* after *death*, so she said to Him, "I know he will rise again in the resurrection at the last day" (John 11:24 NIV).

Then Jesus startled her again. He said, "I am the resurrection and the life. Those who believe in me will live, even though they die; and those who live and believe in me will never die'" (vv. 25–26).

Jesus' words were a shot of spiritual adrenaline. Her heart started racing. Her hope level increased. Her mind became alert. Her vision improved. She saw Jesus in a new light. She saw Him as more than a friend and a miracle worker, she saw Him as the Messiah.

That's why when Jesus asked Martha, "Do you believe this?," she could confidently answer, "Yes, Lord! . . . I do believe that you are the Messiah, the Son of God, who was to come into the world" (vv. 26, 27). Jesus was the One the Jews had been looking for, and yet He was still very much their friend. This was obvious when He entered into the grief experience with Martha and Mary.

SHARED GRIEF

How very touching and comforting it is to have someone to grieve with you when you are experiencing loss, someone who really understands what you are going through. Jesus was deeply moved by what the sisters were feeling, so much so that He wept. But He wasn't going to leave them comfortless. He said, "Let's go to the tomb."

At the tomb, Jesus said, "Take the stone away!" (John 11:39).

Martha objected. "There will be a bad smell, Lord. He has been buried four days!" (v. 39). Practicality was starting to get in the way of Martha's faith so Jesus helped her. He reminded her of what was possible. He said to her, "Didn't I tell you that you would see God's glory if you believed?" (v. 40). In other words, "Hold on, Martha. Your faith was so confident just a short time ago. Don't let up now. Keep on believing." And she did.

Martha watched as the stone was removed from the tomb entrance. She heard Jesus pray, and then heard Him say in a loud voice, "Lazarus, come out!" (v. 43).

Lazarus came out of the tomb, his hands and feet wrapped in grave cloths, and with a cloth around his face. Jesus said, "Untie him, . . . and let him go" (v. 44). The cloths that had kept his body bound in the tomb were unwrapped to reveal an alive, fully functioning Lazarus. The cloth around his face was removed allowing Martha and the others to see the incredulous look on his face. This miracle was so outstanding, so unusual, that it was hard to grasp. Martha kept trying to get her head around the fact that her brother, who had been dead, was now alive. She was overwhelmed with gratitude for what Jesus had done.

Now what about us? Can we expect the same kind of miracle in our lives? Should we expect Jesus to do for us what He did in response to Martha's faith? The premise of this book has been: the surprising things Jesus said—and still says—to women. Jesus' words, "I am the resurrection and the life" (v. 25), were a surprise to Martha because it was so unexpected. Nothing like this miracle had been a part of her experience. Her brother who was dead was given a new life. When Jesus says to us, "I am the resurrection and the life," can we count on the same thing happening if we have faith? What do Jesus' words to Martha say to us?

RESURRECT WHAT?

The most prominent aspect of Jesus' claim is the resurrection. He said, "I am the resurrection" (John 11:25). For a resurrection to occur, there must have been a death.

In Lazarus's case, a physical death occurred from which he was resurrected, but I would hesitate to claim Jesus' words in this kind of occurrence today. Neither do I see other Christians doing this by expecting the dead person they're mourning to be given his or her physical life back.

We have stories of people who die for a brief time and then return to the land of the living. I love reading these stories, but I don't know if the people were appropriating Jesus' claim when their deaths and revivals occurred. Besides, these people will still die a physical death. Even Lazarus, as miraculous as his restoration was, still eventually died, so there has to be more to Jesus' claim. There has to be something with wider applicability, and there is: the spiritual deaths we experience. We may find ourselves in situations so bleak or overwhelming that our human spirit feels as if it has died. At these times, we need a resurrection.

In his commentary on John, William Barclay tells about a young man who got into trouble, bad trouble. "Nobody knew about it—but God knew about it. He felt guilty; he felt his life was ruined; he felt he could never face his family although they need never know; he felt he had killed himself and he was a dead man."[4] He got involved in a small-group Bible study where they were studying John 11, and he found himself in Lazarus's story. As a result, he came alive. He said,

"I know that this resurrection Jesus was talking about is real here and now, for He has raised me from death to life."[5] His troubles weren't over but neither was his life. He had a hard road ahead of him, but his sin was forgiven and his sense of guilt erased. His spirit was revived.

Just as sin may cause spiritual death, an endless string of misfortunes or disappointments can too. Our zest and vitality for life dissipates. Inertia sets in. We just don't feel like doing much of anything. We think, *What's the use? We'll just get knocked down again*. The chronically unemployed or even some retired people may come to feel this way. *There's just nothing out there for me; my life is over*.

I experienced a death of hope when I was depressed. In writing about my experience in *Understanding a Woman's Depression*, I described myself as "a female version of Lazarus."[6] The grave cloths of self-defeat, despair, and purposelessness had wrapped themselves around me suffocating the Brenda within. To get over depression, the grave cloths had to be unwrapped so Brenda could live again.

So when Jesus says, "I am the resurrection," to us, it is as if He is saying, "If you have lost all that makes life worth living, I can make it worthwhile. If you are filled with inertia, I can restore your vitality. If you have sinned to the point that your life looks unredeemable, I can redeem your situation. No person is ever so corrupt, so far down in the gutter, so controlled by sin as to be without hope. Just as I re-created the body of the decaying Lazarus, I can re-create you."

Jesus' claim, though, isn't just about death. In addition to being the resurrection, He is life.

"I AM . . . LIFE"

When we commit ourselves to Jesus, when we take His words to heart and live by them, a certain quality of life becomes ours. On another occasion, Jesus described this life as an abundant one.[7] This means life for the earnest believer is more than breathing. You feel something besides your physical heart throbbing within. You feel the movement of the Holy Spirit, and you feel fully alive. Your life is a vibrant one and a continuous one.

Jesus amplified His statement that He is the resurrection and the life by saying, "Those who believe in me will live, even though they die; and those who live and believe in me will never die" (John 11:25–26). The "whoever" indicates that a vibrant life is possible for all believers. This life begins with real belief and continues on through eternity. It isn't interrupted by physical death, so in that sense, we never die. The spiritual part of us—the part that experiences the abundant life—lives on. This is a truth we can hold on to when we greet mourners in a funeral home or stand by them at the cemetery. It can comfort us as we walk through the valley of the shadow of death. Sometimes, though, we may need some help in holding on to this truth just as Jesus had to help Martha.

THE BELIEF KEY

When Jesus said to Martha that He was the resurrection and the life, He asked her, "Do you believe this?" (John 11:26 NIV). She responded with the most dramatic confession up to this point in John's Gospel. She said, "Lord, I believe that You are the Christ, the Son of God, who is to come into the world" (v. 27 NKJV).

What confidence! What faith! Yet when they got to Lazarus's tomb, when Jesus ordered the stone at the entrance to be taken away, Martha said, "There will be a bad smell, Lord. He has been buried four days!" (v. 39). Reality was raising its ugly head, threatening her faith.

Jesus, though, encouraged her. "Jesus said to her, 'Didn't I tell you that you would see God's glory if you *believed?*'" (v. 40, author's italics). In other words, "Martha, don't give up now. Hold on, we're almost there, and you're going to see something glorious."

Seeing the glorious is another attribute of the life Jesus gives. When we cling to this aspect of His nature, we'll have eyes to see Him reveal Himself. We'll recognize His involvement in our lives, and we'll see Him redeem what appears to be hopeless situations.

Jesus' question reminded Martha—and reminds us—that *belief* is the key to experiencing "the resurrection and the life." This doesn't mean an intellectual belief. It's not answering a test question: Jesus is the resurrection and the life. True or false? On a test, you could answer "True" without ever believing it enough to act on it. The kind of belief Jesus is talking about means accepting what He says so strongly that it permeates our being and determines our actions. This kind of belief enables Jesus to resurrect us. This kind of belief enables us to experience a vibrant life. It's what I call "hard" believing, not "easy" believing.

Numerous times I've had to do some "hard" believing. One of those times was when I was depressed. While several factors contributed to my depression, behind it all was thinking God did not have a purpose for my life. While I got over depression's physical symptoms, I couldn't get over the spiritual part until I "unwrapped the grave cloths." I began acknowledging that He had a purpose for me. Every morning I affirmed this truth in my prayers and then acted as if it were true throughout the day. Eventually, the acting part was no longer necessary because true belief arrived, and I was resurrected. I was able to experience the abundant life once again.

Like Martha we are all influenced by reality. What we see and hear, the stage of life we're in, our physical health, our monetary situation, and any number of other things can gnaw away at our faith. We may even become so distressed that we think our friend, Jesus, is not going to "show up" for us, but He will although it may not be in the way we expect. It may be more than we expect. Like Martha we may discover that Jesus is more than a friend and we may be able to see God's glory in a spectacular way. I don't want to miss out on something like that, do you? That's why I am going to answer the question, *Do you believe?* with a hearty yes! What's your answer?

FROM MIND TO HEART

When have you felt like Martha and Mary — that if Jesus had shown up when you needed Him, things might not have happened as they did?

What does Jesus' statement, "I am the resurrection and the life," mean to you?

Jesus promised Martha that if she believed, she would see the glory of God. How will belief enable us to see God reveal Himself?

Was the resurrection of Lazarus the same as the Resurrection of Jesus?

How would you describe the life Jesus offers?

What's the difference between "easy" believing and "hard" believing?

7/20 PART IV

HE CONSOLED HOW?

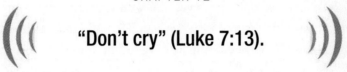

"Don't cry" (Luke 7:13).

OCCASIONALLY YOU MAY WISH YOU COULD CURL UP IN YOUR MOTHER'S lap, cry your heart out, and hear her say, "There, there now, baby. Don't cry. Everything's going to be all right." Not that you would ever admit this desire to anyone! After all, we are competent, responsible adults, but still there may come a time of sorrow so keen that you long for a mother's comfort. You want to be consoled like you were as a child. You want to be reassured that everything is going to be all right, and then you'll pull yourself together! A woman may feel this way when her marriage breaks up, when a child disappoints her, or when she experiences a deep loss such as the widow of Nain experienced.

WHO?

We know little about this nameless woman who lived in Nain, a town in the hill country of Galilee. We know enough, though, from her story in Luke 7:11–17 that we feel for her. She was a widow, and her only son had died. Even if the Bible didn't say *"only* son," we would understand her grief. The loss of a child is very difficult.

If she had daughters, the Bible doesn't say. The impression given is that she was left totally alone, but perhaps this is to emphasize that her economic support was gone. Most women were financially dependent on the males in their lives, and now with her son's death, her means of support was gone. Unless she remarried, which was unlikely, since she was probably past the childbearing years, or unless relatives came to her aid, she was without resources.

Her loss, though, was about more than economic security. She would miss him and the spark he brought to her household. She would miss his male perspective. She would yearn for his presence. She would miss his future—the woman he would marry, the children he would have. When her thoughts trailed on like this, the pain was almost more than she could bear. She wanted to curl up and hide from the world, but she couldn't because her son needed to be buried.

The widow's tears flowed freely as she made her way to the burial caves in the rocky hills just outside of Nain. She had been to the caves before to bury her husband, but this time her loss was worse. When her husband died, she still had her son. Now she felt very alone even though many "people of the city" (Luke 7:12 KJV) went with her to the burial tombs.

TO THE CEMETERY

Many people accompanied her because they sympathized with the depth of her loss; others did it because it was the customary thing to do. Professional mourners may have been part of the mix adding the sounds of flutes and cymbals to the shrill cries of grief as the entourage made their way to the tombs.

The dead body was carried in a wicker stretcherlike basket, although many Bible translations say coffin. It was not a coffin, for coffins were not used in Galilee at this time. Instead, long wickerwork baskets were used. The body was wrapped and placed on the long wicker basket and carried to the burial site.

Amid the noise of the flutes, the cymbals, and the wailing, the widow's weeping could be heard. Wringing her hands and moaning, she lamented over and over again, "What am I going to do? Whatever am I going to do without my son?"

Her support, her hope, and her joy had been taken from her. Her future looked bleak, and it was until Jesus came along.

THEN JESUS CAME

At this time, Jesus was touring Galilee with His disciples. As He healed and preached, the number of followers increased. By the time he neared Nain a large crowd was with Him. Together they climbed up hills, past rocky tombs where the dead were laid. At Nain's city gate, the two crowds—the one with the widow and the one with Jesus—merged.

Jesus' eyes quickly took in the whole scene.

He saw the bier.

He saw the bier carriers.

He saw the crowd.

He heard the flutes, the cymbals, and the wailing.

He saw the woman who was the center of it all.

He saw her tears, and He heard her crying.

This picture needed no headlines, no title, or no explanation. A woman was hurting, and Jesus noticed. He said to her, "Don't cry" (Luke 7:13).

Those standing close enough to hear were probably puzzled. How could a woman not cry at a time like this? Wouldn't weeping be a natural response to such a fresh and deep loss?

Actually, Jesus' words were meant to comfort. His saying, "Don't cry," was Jesus' way of saying, "There, there now. It's going to be all right." Like a good, understanding mother, Jesus perceived what she was going through, and He determined to make it better. We know this because "his heart was filled with pity for her" (Luke 7:13).

THE COMPASSION OF CHRIST

The Greek word behind "filled with pity for her," "he had compassion on her" (KJV), and "his heart went out to her" (NIV) is *splagchnizesthai*. It is the strongest word in the Greek language for compassionate pity. "The *splagchna* are *the bowels*; and *splagchnizesthai* means *to be moved to the very depths of one's being*."[1]

On other occasions besides this one, the gospel writers use this word to describe Jesus' concern for people.

- "When he saw the multitudes, he was moved with compassion on them, because they fainted, and were scattered abroad, as sheep having no shepherd" (Matthew 9:36 KJV).
- When he tried to get away to a lonely place after hearing the news of John the Baptist's death, He was moved by compassion for "a great multitude" that surrounded Him, and "he healed their sick" (Matthew 14:14 KJV). See also Mark 6:34.
- When more than 4,000 gathered to hear Him preach for three days, Jesus said to His disciples, "I have compassion on the multitude, because they continue with me now three days, and have nothing to eat: and I will not send them away fasting, lest they faint in the way" (Matthew 15:32 KJV). See also Mark 8:2.
- When two blind men from the side of the road cried out to him to have mercy on them, "Jesus had compassion on them, and touched their eyes: and immediately their eyes received sight, and they followed him" (Matthew 20:34 KJV).
- When a begging leper said to Jesus, "If you want to, you can make me clean" (Mark 1:40), He, "moved with compassion, put forth his hand, and touched him, and saith unto him, I will; be thou clean" (v. 41 KJV).

Jesus was moved to the depths of His being by a grieving woman, a leaderless crowd, a hungry crowd, blind men, and a begging leper. And in these instances, His compassion moved Him to action, even to the point of breaking some rules the Jewish religious leaders considered to be important.

RULE-BREAKING COMPASSION

As the crowds merged, everyone assumed the march to the burial tomb would continue. This was what would normally happen. If you saw a group of mourners on the way to a cemetery, you joined the march even if you didn't know the people. It was the customary thing to do like pulling over to the side of the road when cars in a funeral procession pass by.

Consequently, everyone expected Jesus to fall in line, but He surprised them. He halted the procession. He did this by touching the bier, prompting some to gasp, *What's He doing? Who does He think he is? He has no right to stop a funeral parade!*

To stop a parade of mourners by touching the bier was a nervy thing to do. From our viewpoint, Jesus had every right to halt a funeral procession because He was the Son of God, but the mourners didn't recognize Him as such.[2] Some mourners possibly hadn't even heard of Him, and they were startled by His action. Touching a bier was a no-no.

If a person touched a dead body or anything the body had touched, he or she became unclean for seven days.[3] Cleansing was a complicated process that required ceremonial purification before a person could return to the synagogue for worship. The bearers of the corpse had to experience such defilement in order to bury the dead. Jesus knew the rules, but without hesitation He touched the untouchable. Jesus touched the bier, and in this one gesture brought the noisy group to a silent halt.

At Jesus' touch, the men carrying the bier stopped and stood still. So did the crowd. All eyes were on Jesus as He took command of the situation. An eerie quiet followed as everyone wondered, *What's going to happen now?*

THE SECOND SURPRISE

With authority Jesus spoke to the wrapped body, "Young man! Get up, I tell you!" (Luke 7:14). And he did! He was alive! Physical death is so final that no one expected this to happen. When you are on your way to bury a dead person, you don't expect a resurrection.

The young man sat up, ripped off the cloth he had been wrapped in, and began to talk. Don't you wonder what he said? Did he say what it was like to be dead? Did he talk about what caused his death? Did he comfort his mother? Did he say, "I'm sorry you had to experience this sorrow?" Was the son ecstatic about his return to the land of the living?

What was the mother's reaction when "Jesus gave him back to" her (v. 15)? Did she shout "Hallelujah!"? Did she fall on her knees and profusely thank Jesus? Did she grab hold of her son and cling to him?

We don't know what the young man or the mother said. The Bible doesn't tell us, but it does tell what the people of Nain said.

HOW THE PEOPLE RESPONDED

The onlookers were awestruck by this man who had the audacity to stop a funeral march, who told a grieving widow/mother not to cry, who touched a bier, and who brought a dead man back to life. Not a typical everyday experience!

This miracle filled them with fear—a good kind of fear. We mostly think of fear as anxiety and frustration in response to something that is happening such as flood waters rising, disturbing physical symptoms, a fugitive loose in the neighborhood, etc. We are filled with dread and apprehension as to what might happen. But fear also has a positive sense when it means amazement, reverence, and awe. Positive fear may also include a mysterious element, mysterious in the sense of something happening that defies human explanation. Bringing someone back from the dead certainly defies human explanation! They had never seen anything like this![4]

Their fear led them to say, "A great prophet has appeared among us!" (Luke 7:16). Someone who could bring back a young man from death must be a prophet. When they said this, they were probably thinking of the miracle-working prophets Elisha and Elijah.

Elisha raised the son of a Shunammite woman who had been hospitable to him.[5] From time to time, he stayed with this woman and her husband. Eventually, the Shunammite woman provided a comfortable, permanent place for the prophet. Elisha wished to do something in return for her gracious hospitality. She had no children, so Elisha prophesied that in the next year she would hold a son in her arms. She and her husband conceived, and a child was born. Later when the child was older, he fell ill while working with his father in the fields; he died in his mother's lap. The mother sought Elisha's help. Elisha went to the boy, prayed for him, and the boy recovered.

Elijah raised the son of the Widow of Zarephath.[6] Elijah, on the run from the godless Queen Jezebel, was sheltered by this poor widow and her son. Elijah stayed with them for two years, and God miraculously provided food for them. The boy became ill and died. Elijah took the boy to the upper room where he was staying and laid him on his own bed. Then he stretched himself out on the child three times and prayed to God to save the boy. God heard Elijah's prayer, and the boy was revived. Elijah took the child to his mother and said, "See, your son lives!" (1 Kings 17:23 NKJV).

"Then the woman said to Elijah, 'Now by this I know that you are a man of God, and that the word of the LORD in your mouth is the truth'" (v. 24 NKJV).

The crowd at Nain had a similar reaction. They concluded that God had "come to save his people!" (Luke 7:16). They couldn't help but talk about what happened. "This news about Jesus went out through all the country and the surrounding territory" (v. 17).

I hope it has spread to you too. If you are hurting deeply, I want you to realize Jesus may say to you what He said to the widow of Nain, "Don't cry. Don't go on weeping. I'm here to comfort. Everything's going to be all right." You may not even need to ask Him to act on your behalf because the God who speaks also sees.

"THOU GOD SEEST ME"

I'll never forget the day I stood in front of a classroom of college students and read aloud the story of Hagar crying in the wilderness. Hagar was the "second wife," the concubine, to Abraham.[7] His first wife, Sarah,[8] had arranged for her maid servant Hagar to have sexual relations with Abraham so they could have a child. Sarah and Abraham had no children.

After she became pregnant, Hagar, who didn't have a choice in all of this, ran away. She ended up alone in the wilderness with no way to provide for herself and her child. Realizing what a predicament she was in, Hagar cried and cried. God saw her weeping and sent an angel to minister to her. Hagar was elated that the God of the universe saw her. She exclaimed, "Thou God seest me" (Genesis 16:13 KJV).

As I read aloud, I suddenly realized that Hagar didn't seek God's help. God saw her! She didn't have to ask for Him to act. This realization blew my mind because so much of what I had been taught in the Christian life was about our approaching God. Yet here was a woman who wasn't seeking, who was alone and troubled in the wilderness, and God saw her. He met her need without her having to ask for His help. This was a memorable day for me because it took some of the pressure off of living the Christian life.

Like Hagar, the widow of Nain didn't ask for Jesus' help. There's no mention of her having faith. There was no request on her part, no pleading, no asking, no trying to get her request phrased just right, and no asking the crowd to intercede on her behalf. Jesus acted on His own initiative. He saw her grief, understood her loss, and was moved to help her. He acted compassionately and gave her son back to her.

While we want to always make sure we approach God with our needs and be mindful of how we do it, it is comforting to know that it's not all up to us. Hundreds of years ago, the prophet Isaiah pictured God as a mother who comforts.[9] That picture came true in

Jesus Christ. Like a mother, He is aware, He sees, He speaks, and He comforts. Every day I remind myself of this by saying to Him, "Your eyes are open to the ways of men and women, and I know you see me today." I can rely on this because the God who speaks is the God who sees.

FROM MIND TO HEART

In telling the widow of Nain not to cry, is Jesus saying to us not to cry about things that trouble and grieve us?

How does Jesus today give back to those who have lost?

How does Jesus return a son to his mother?

How does Jesus return a daughter to her?

When has Jesus spoken to you in such a way that you felt comforted?

When might you find yourself saying about Jesus, "Now I know that you are a man of God and that the Lord really speaks through you!" (1 Kings 17:24)?

What aspect of Jesus' nature does this incident highlight?

CHAPTER 13

"Woman, behold, your son!"
(John 19:26 NASB).

A FRIEND AND I OFTEN TALKED AND PRAYED ABOUT HER ADOPTING A child. In one of our many conversations, Megan said, "I don't want a child that will break my heart." I said, "Oh, hon, that's a given." Whether they are biological or adopted, children break our hearts, sometimes in small ways and sometimes in big ways. Even Mary, the mother of Jesus, was not exempt.

HEARTBREAKING RUMORS

After the wedding in Cana (see John 2), Jesus and His disciples went back to Judea, and Mary and her other sons returned home to Nazareth. As Mary reflected on the wedding, she was certain of Jesus' ability to perform miracles. Jesus would be able to help many people. His future was bright. He would do well; He would be respected as He traveled in Galilee and Judea, preaching, teaching, and healing.

And He did do well. Mary heard rave reviews of the good things Jesus did as He healed the sick and exorcized demons. People clamored to hear Jesus' messages. Mary's heart swelled with pride when she heard people talking about Him. What a good Son! He was so dedicated to helping people.

After a while, the rumors took on another tone. His miracles changed people's lives and revealed Jesus' compassion, but they also caused Him to get a lot of attention. Many people followed Him just to see what would happen next. The size of the crowds worried

Roman officials. They regarded anyone who could attract thousands as a possible dissident, and Mary knew they had no qualms about punishing people they saw as a threat to the empire.

Jewish officials, especially the religious leaders, also became alarmed because people began suggesting that Jesus was the Messiah. When they checked Him out, they heard Jesus say things that challenged their sacred rules. This raised their ire and they determined to find a way to get rid of Him. They joined the crowds surrounding Jesus, hoping to catch Him doing or saying something for which they could arrest Him. The religious leaders credited his miracle-working power to Beelzebul, the chief of demons. Some people even said Jesus had "gone mad" (Mark 3:21).

When comments like these reached Mary, she was flabbergasted. She was also frightened. "That's my son they are talking about!" Her maternal instincts kicked in, and she said to herself, "We'll just see about this." She said to Jesus' brothers and sisters, "Let's go find Jesus and bring Him home."

HEARTBREAKING WORDS

When they found Jesus, He was in a house with a crowd "sitting around" Him (Mark 3:32). The crowd prevented them from going in, so Mary and her children "sent in a message, asking for him" (v. 31). They waited expectantly. Picking up on the message's content as it passed from person to person, the crowd said to Jesus, "Look, your mother and your brothers and sisters are outside, and they want you" (v. 32).

Jesus shocked His family and maybe some of the crowd, too, when He "answered, 'Who is my mother? Who are my brothers?' He looked at the people sitting around him and said, 'Look! Here are my mother and my brothers! Whoever does what God wants is my brother, my sister, my mother'" (vv. 33–35).[1]

While we know—and hopefully understand—the spiritual principle in Jesus' words (all human relationships must be subordinated to the higher spiritual relationships of the kingdom of God), Mary felt like a knife had been plunged into her heart. The words made her recall what Simeon had said to her when Jesus was a baby. As proud new parents, Joseph and Mary had taken Baby Jesus to the Temple in Jerusalem. Simeon, who was a fixture there, spoke regarding Jesus' future, and he also referenced Mary's future. He said, "Sorrow, like a sharp sword, will break your own heart" (Luke 2:35).

Now with Jesus' refusal to see them, Simeon's prophecy was coming true. Mary's journey home was a somber one. She had a lot of sorting out to do. Why couldn't Jesus at least have come outside and said hello? How could He ignore them? She wanted Him to serve God, to be helpful and kind, but why should serving God interfere with family? Couldn't He be a good son and also serve God? She wanted Jesus to be safe. Why couldn't He just come home? He had been a good carpenter. Why couldn't He serve God as a carpenter?

Back home, she eventually mellowed as she remembered something else Simeon had said. He spoke of Jesus as being "a light to reveal" God's "will to the Gentiles and bring glory to [God's] people Israel" (v. 32). Quite possibly this was what was happening, and if it was, then she wanted to cooperate. She might not have a family connection with Jesus any longer, but she could be a supportive follower. Her other sons didn't see it that way (John 7:3–8). They didn't see Jesus as revealing God's will so Mary and her still nearby sons parted ways. They stayed in Nazareth, and Mary went to Jerusalem.

HEARTBREAK IN JERUSALEM

Mary apparently joined up with a group of women in Galilee who were followers of Jesus and supportive of His ministry.[2] Exactly when this might have happened, we don't know, but we do know she was with them in Jerusalem in Judea. They had followed Jesus there because they heard the hostility against Jesus in Jerusalem was at an all-time high.

Once there, they learned Jesus had been arrested and condemned to die by crucifixion. The women went to the crucifixion scene, not that there was anything they could do to stop the Romans from carrying out this despicable act, but they could "be there." They could show Jesus their love and support.

The list of named Galilean women varies from gospel to gospel. John's gospel specifically states four that were present at the Cross: Mary (Jesus' mother), Mary's sister, the wife of Clopas, and Mary Magdalene. They all hurt to see Jesus suffer, but none hurt as much as Mary.

Tears slipped down her cheeks and kept falling as she observed Jesus on the Cross. She could hardly bear to look but neither could she stop looking. While in some deep, mysterious way this appeared to be God's will for Jesus, still this was *her* son, the one she had given birth to and who had lived with her for 30 years. To see Him like this, dying a criminal's death, nailed to a cross, experiencing excruciating pain, and being ridiculed was almost more than she could bear.

While watching her son die, you would think that would be all Mary could think about, but it wasn't. Isn't it amazing that even when you are deeply grieving that other thoughts creep in? You wonder, *How could I think about that at a time like this?* I remember when my father died, when we returned to the family home after the funeral, I kept hearing my authoritative father say, "Turn out the lights"; "Shut the door"; "You girls stop giggling now"; etc. I thought, *Where are these 'orders' from my childhood coming from and why now?*

But grief — and thinking! — are never simple. As Mary grieved, some emotional residue from the incident at the crowded house in Galilee surfaced. She still felt the sting of Jesus' not taking the time to talk with her and His siblings. It came from that family part of being a mother. No matter where your children are or what they are doing, you still want to be family. You still want to hold them close, to have times together. You at least want them to speak to you! And Jesus had refused even to acknowledge their presence. She wondered, *Did He still feel that way? Did He still want to be disassociated with His family?*

Another intrusive thought popped into her head as she thought of family. What was ahead for her? This little band of women would probably break up. She wasn't on the best of terms with her other sons because she believed in Jesus, and they didn't (John 7:5). If Jesus had stayed in Nazareth, her care would have been His responsibility. In Jewish culture, the oldest son was supposed to take care of the widowed mother. As she saw His life end, she wondered if her own life were ending too. *Whatever was she going to do?*

Even though she was with other women at the Cross, she felt alone. Even though she had been "on the road" with them, she kept her troubling thoughts to herself. This wasn't the time or the place for sharing. She felt forlorn and abandoned, but Mary was in for a surprise. Jesus would say something that would change everything.

WHAT JESUS SAID

Great physical pain can totally dominate a person's attention, so it is a marvel that Jesus "saw his mother and the disciple he loved standing there" (John 19:26). He did not see her as just another person in the crowd; He saw his mother. He saw how she loved Him. He also saw her need and noticed her forlorn appearance. He realized what the days ahead would be like for her. He wanted her to be protected and looked after so He arranged for her care. He said, "Woman, *behold,* your son!" (NASB, author's italics) as He nodded toward John.

Jesus didn't call her name, but Mary knew the message was for her. That "behold" got her attention. He was looking at her. His words had an urgency to them, and an intensity that made it almost a command. Her heart fluttered. He was aware that she was present! In the crowd, in all the activity, Jesus saw *her*, spoke to her, and resolved her dilemma.

She looked in the direction Jesus' head had turned when He spoke. The nod was toward John, the only apostle present. She heard Jesus say to John, "Behold, your mother!" (v. 27 NASB), and she knew as surely as you can know anything that she was being taken care of. Jesus did care! They were still family! She was amazed, and so was I as I studied Jesus' words to Mary.

In the last moments of His life, and in the midst of excruciating pain, Jesus thought of His brokenhearted mother and arranged for her future care. Even when saving a lost world, even when experiencing torment so terrible that He felt abandoned by God, He remembered His mother and made provision for her.

Jesus died for the whole world in an act of supreme self-sacrifice, and yet with the salvation of the world hanging in the balance, Jesus had "a mind lifted above himself, serene and calm enough to think, and pray, and plan, for others."[3]

At a time when Jesus was suffering, He disregarded His personal agony. He performed His duties as a son. His words to Mary and John show Jesus having a ministry right up to the end of His life, and what's more, His ministry continues. And in that role, He may want to get our attention. He may want to say to us "Woman, behold" just as He did to Mary.

"WOMAN, BEHOLD"

In both the King James Version and the New American Standard Version of the Bible, the word "behold" in John 19:27 is used in Jesus' words to Mary and to John, as it should be. "Behold" catches the literal meaning of what Jesus said. It's an Old English word used numerous times in the King James Version of the Bible, but it's a word seldom used today. Maybe that's why some Bible versions do not use it. For example, the New International Version reads, "Woman, here is your son," and the Good News Translation says, "He is your son," which I think weakens what Jesus was saying to both Mary and John. This kind of life-changing, life-enhancing pronouncement calls for something more powerful and dramatic, and "behold" fills the bill. "Behold" is an imperative verb that expresses the intensity of Jesus' desire. Time was running out, and He needed to get the attention of Mary and John and make sure they acted on what He had to say, and they did. "From that time the disciple took her to live in his home."

In the spiritual sense, "behold" indicates hope and possibilities where you can't see any.

BEHOLD, I AM AWARE OF YOU.

BEHOLD, YOU ARE NOT FORGOTTEN.

BEHOLD, THERE ARE SOLUTIONS TO YOUR PROBLEMS.

BEHOLD, IT IS NOT OVER UNTIL IT IS OVER.

To Mary, Jesus gave her a solution where she didn't see one. In other words, Jesus was saying, "I will not leave you like this. I care, and I'm helping. I have a solution for you, one you hadn't thought of." Actually, He gave her more than a solution and immediate comfort. He gave her a family.

In John's care, Mary was absorbed into a wider family—the group of Christians in Jerusalem who met together in the Upper Room after Jesus' ascension. They did this to follow the instructions Jesus gave the apostles at one of His resurrection appearances. He said, "Do not leave Jerusalem, but wait for the gift . . . my Father promised. John baptized with water, but in a few days you will be baptized with the Holy Spirit" (Acts 1:4–5).

In their "wait" for the Holy Spirit, the disciples met together "frequently to pray as a group" (v. 14). Some women, Mary, and Jesus' brothers were a part of this group. How had this happened? Had the wider spiritual family helped unite Mary's family? Had she been instrumental in bringing them in? Or had the brothers picked up on what was happening and come to Jerusalem in repentance for not believing earlier? We don't know, but we do know Mary had a family, and my friend, Megan, gained one too.

7/26

THE GIFT OF FAMILY

Megan and I prayed fervently for a child to grace her childless home. As foster children came and went, as applications were made to adoption agencies, we wondered who would be "the one." At times, we got discouraged, but we prayed continuing to listen for Jesus to say, "Behold, this is the child for you," and one day, He did. A seven-year-old girl became a part of Megan's household.

Just as Jesus said "behold" to Mary—and to Megan—there's also the possibility that He will say "behold" to us. We don't have to be mothers to have mixed emotions, to be in a mental fog where our vision is cloudy and our future appears grim. A time comes for all of us when we experience heartbreak, and it did right on schedule for Megan.

Adopting a seven-year-old meant Megan's child came with a past. One day Megan came to my house looking very somber. Megan said, "Remember when you said that it's a given that your child will break your heart?"

"Yes, I remember. What's wrong?"

Tears began to flow as Megan told me about a problem she was having with her daughter because of her past. It broke Megan's heart to know what her daughter had endured and what this might mean for her future. As we discussed this, we put ourselves in a position to listen for Jesus to say, "Behold, it's going to be all right. I'm going to see you through this." We prayed.

Many of us go through times of vulnerability when we feel like we are losing our grip on life and faith. Whether or not we are mothers, we may feel disconnected, confused, weak, helpless, insecure, fearful, hurt, and defenseless. God's actions—or lack of action—may confuse us. Life's sunlight fades and sadness engulfs us. This is when we need to pause, meditate on Jesus' love so powerfully displayed at the Cross, and listen closely. If we're quiet enough, we may hear Him say to us as He did to Mary, "Woman, behold! I have a solution for you."

FROM MIND TO HEART

Why did Mary want to rescue Jesus?

How does family interfere with serving the Lord?

How does family help in serving the Lord?

Why were Jesus' words from the Cross to Mary a surprise?

Why might quiet be necessary to hear Jesus say, "Woman, behold!"?

How can we quiet ourselves to hear Jesus speak to us?

CHAPTER 14

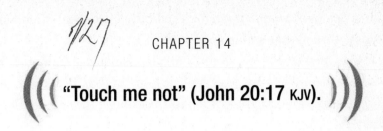

"Touch me not" (John 20:17 KJV).

SOMETIMES WHEN LOVED ONES DIE UNEXPECTEDLY OR IN TRAGIC circumstances, you catch yourself wondering, *Did it really happen? Is he or she really gone?* You may deal with this by replaying the scene over and over in your mind. You may deal with it by talking to yourself or to others, or you may reassure yourself by visiting the gravesite. This is what the Galilean women did on Sunday morning after Jesus' death on Friday. They headed to the tomb.

WAS IT FOR REAL?

The Galilean women were women who supported Jesus and the disciples as He traveled throughout Galilee. They had followed Him to Jerusalem and were present at the foot of the Cross when Jesus was crucified. They watched their healer, leader, teacher, and friend suffer excruciating pain. All the while, the women stood helplessly by wishing there was something they could do—anything to help this One they loved so much, but there wasn't. They observed His final breath and saw a Roman soldier pierce His side, proving He was indeed dead.

They were relieved when Joseph, a rich Jewish man of Arimathaea, and Nicodemus, the Pharisee who visited Jesus at night, claimed His body.

The women assisted Joseph and Nicodemus in receiving the battered body and cleansing it. Joseph wrapped Jesus in a clean sheet.

Linen strips were wrapped around the body. Spices that Nicodemus provided were placed within their folds.

The women went with Joseph and Nicodemus to a tomb that had never been used. They saw Joseph place Jesus' body in it (see Matthew 27:60). Joseph "rolled a great stone to the door of the sepulchre, and departed" (KJV).

Mary Magdalene and another Mary, also a part of the Galilean group, sat watching "over against the sepulchre" (v. 61 KJV). The women wondered, *Could this really be happening? Is Jesus really dead?* The moment was seared in their memory as they "beheld the sepulchre, and how his body was laid" (Luke 23:55 KJV).

Finally as darkness started to fall, they returned to Jerusalem and joined other women there who were preparing spices and perfumed ointments for ministering to Jesus' body. This was something relatives did for their deceased loved ones. They believed this slowed down the decay process, and they purposely anointed the body while the deceased's spirit still hovered.

The Galilean women would have liked to have immediately done this for Jesus as soon as Joseph placed Him in the tomb or the first thing Saturday morning, but the Sabbath began at sundown Friday and would continue until sundown Saturday. During the Sabbath all work ceased, and work included anointing a dead body with spices and ointments, so the women waited.

Saturday was a long, frustrating day for the Galilean women. From time to time throughout the day, one of them would shake her head and say, "I still can't believe it. Jesus is dead?" As soon as one of them said it, their minds returned to Friday and the awful nightmare they had experienced. They needed confirmation that what they had seen and witnessed on Friday had not been a figment of their imagination. Had it been real? Was He really dead?

Besides dealing with disbelief, they also felt an urgency to do something. How could you not minister to a loved one and a friend? One thing they could do was to anoint His body. If they could just get to the tomb, open it, touch Him, and caress His arms and hands with perfume, they would feel so much better, but they had to wait for the Sabbath to end. As soon as they could on Sunday morning, when it was just barely light enough to see, the women with their spices and ointment headed for the tomb with Mary Magdalene leading the way.

 MARY WHO?

More than one Mary was a part of this group of Galilean women whom Jesus had "healed of evil spirits and infirmities" (Luke 8:2 KJV). We learned about some of the other Marys in chapter 12. Mary Magdalene is distinguished from the others by referencing her home town. She came from Magdala, a town located on the shores of the Sea of Galilee, hence she is called Mary Magdalene.

When Jesus healed Mary Magdalene, He healed her of severe demon possession. Seven demons had been cast out of her. Before her exorcism, Mary contended with the evil spirits within and dealt with the responses of people to her odd behavior. Forces within and without threatened to destroy her, but Jesus set her free. No wonder she became an enthusiastic part of this group who spent their days following Jesus and supporting His ministry.

On Saturday, after Jesus' death on Friday, Mary thought about how Jesus had set her free. How energized and renewed she felt! How her gratitude motivated her to serve Him! She couldn't help but become a loyal follower of Jesus; eventually she became the leader of this group of women. Throughout the day, she replayed experiences the women had with Him as they traveled throughout Galilee, but intertwined with these scenes were images of His death. How heartwrenching it had been to see Jesus crucified! Like some of the other women, she found it hard to believe His death had really happened. She was anxious to get to the tomb, to settle in her mind that He really was gone. When she touched the body again, then she would know for sure. The problem, though, was going to be getting inside the tomb.

THE FORMIDABLE STONE

Tombs in those days were not usually closed by doors. In front of the opening there ran a groove in the ground, and in the groove there ran a stone, circular like a wagon wheel. The stone was wheeled into position to form a door. The stone was very large and heavy, and the Romans sealed the stone to Jesus' tomb to make sure no one would move it (Matthew 27:66).

None of this deterred the women although they discussed the problem as they walked along. "They said among themselves, Who shall roll away the stone from the door of the sepulchre?" (Mark 16:3 KJV). Nevertheless, even without an answer, they continued on. They were intent on their mission. Perhaps the gardener who worked the burial grounds would help them. Somehow they would get the tomb opened.

Mary Magdalene may have become frustrated with the conversation or impatient with their walking pace because she moved on ahead. When she arrived at the burial grounds, Mary gasped, "Oh my!" There was no stone in front of the sepulchre! Mary was astonished to find the entrance clear. The tomb was open!

Fear immediately clutched her throat; something was dreadfully wrong. *What's going on? Had the tomb been broken into? Had Jesus' body been desecrated? Or worse, had it been stolen?*

Mary hastened to tell Peter and John, two of Jesus' apostles. She said, "They have taken the Lord out of the tomb, and we don't know where they have put him" (John 20:2 NIV).

Now they were alarmed! Peter and John rushed to the tomb. Mary followed, but couldn't keep up with them.

John arrived first. He looked in the tomb and discovered Jesus wasn't there. John saw the strips of linen—the ones that had been wrapped around Jesus' body—lying there but did not go in.

Peter, though, went in when he arrived. He, too, saw the strips of linen, and "the burial cloth that had been wrapped around Jesus' head" (vv. 6–7 NIV).

With the realization that the tomb was empty—and yet not fully certain what all this meant—Peter and John returned home. Mary, who had arrived by this time, watched them leave. She couldn't believe Jesus' body was gone. What happened? It was all so puzzling. Where was He? She "stood outside the tomb crying" (v. 11 NIV).

"As she wept, she bent over to look into the tomb and saw two angels in white, seated where Jesus' body had been, one at the head and the other at the foot" (vv. 11–12 NIV).

The angels asked her, "Woman, why are you crying?"

Mary answered, "They have taken my Lord away, and I do not know where they have put him!" "They" could have been those Jews who had been intent on bringing about Jesus' death. She might have been fearful they were going to further inflict Jesus' body. Or "they" could have been grave mongers who spent time in burial places, destroying bodies and robbing graves.

At another time, in another place, the appearance of angels might have been welcomed, but not this day. Angels, they may be, but she had Jesus in mind. Where was He?

NEARER THAN SHE THOUGHT

Mary turned away from the angels. When she did, she saw a person standing there. It was Jesus, but she didn't recognize Him. It's hard to see clearly through tears.

Jesus asked Mary, "Woman, why are you crying? Who is it that you are looking for?"

Now I find His questions surprising. Wouldn't it be obvious to almost anyone why she was crying if she was standing in front of a tomb in a burial ground and it was open? And wouldn't she be looking for the body that was buried in the tomb?

When Jesus saw how distraught and confused Mary was, why didn't He say, "Woman, look at Me. Don't cry. I'm here. I'm Jesus. I'm who you are looking for"? Why wasn't He immediately reassuring instead of asking questions?

Perhaps the questions were needed to help Mary gain control of herself, to stop the tears from falling and to gain some composure so she could grasp what was happening. Sometimes when you are grieving, when tears are fresh and plentiful, it is hard to comprehend reality. Mary needed to pull herself together to fully assess what was happening so she could be a creditable witness. Jesus was going to commission her to be an apostle to the apostles.

GRASPING REALITY

As Mary gained some composure, she concluded the person speaking to her was the gardener. Still thinking someone or some people carried off Jesus' body, she said, "Sir, if you have carried him away, tell me where you have put him, and I will get him" (John 20:15 NIV).

How in the world was Mary going to "get him"? Even if she were a large, strong woman, she wouldn't have enough strength to move dead weight. And if she could, where would she take the body? At the moment, it didn't matter how. This was love speaking. Finding Him and caring for Him was paramount.

Then something precious and totally unexpected happened. The resurrected Jesus spoke. He said one word. He said, "Mary!"

Instant recognition! No one had ever said her name quite like Jesus had, and now here He was before her! Saying her name!

"Rabboni!"[1] she said.

The tears stopped. Her vision cleared. The person in front of her was Jesus! He was right there! He wasn't dead. He was alive! She moved toward Him and embraced Him.

He reacted by saying, "Touch me not" (John 20:17 KJV). Don't touch Him? How could she not touch Him? How could she not express herself at the joy of discovery His aliveness?

TELL, NOT TOUCH

Jesus' telling Mary "Touch me not" is puzzling. Here is a woman who was grieving over the death of her friend, teacher, and healer who saw Him experience a cruel death, and now she joyously learns He's alive. She's relieved! She's delighted! She's happy! Wouldn't touching Him be a natural response?

His words are even more puzzling when you consider that Jesus invited Thomas to touch Him (John 20:27) and to the terrified disciples, He said, "Handle me, and see" (Luke 24:39 KJV).

In Matthew's Gospel, we read that some women "held Him by the feet, and worshipped Him" (Matthew 28:9 KJV). In Mary's case, though, more than a simple touch may have been involved. While John 20:17 in the King James Version reads, "Touch me not," other versions translate the phrase differently. The New International Version and the Good News Translation translate it this way: "Do not hold on to me." This is the more accurate translation because "in the Greek the verb *touch* is a present imperative; and when used as a prohibition"[2] gives the meaning of "Stop touching Me" or "Do not cling to Me."

Jesus didn't want Mary to cling to Him although you could certainly understand why she would want to. Since she had lost Him once, she wanted to hold on to Him and never let Him go. She needed to learn, though, that their relationship would not pick up where it left off. Actually, this was something all of the disciples would have to learn. A new way of relating to Jesus was coming into existence.

We can better understand Jesus' saying, "Do not hold on to me" when we read the rest of what Jesus said to Mary. He went on to explain, "for I have not yet ascended to the Father. Go instead to my brothers and tell them, 'I am ascending to my Father and your Father, to my God and your God'" (John 20:17 NIV).

Jesus' words "not yet ascended" and "I am ascending" indicate that He was involved in a process, a process that had not yet been fully completed. It would culminate with Jesus' ascension and the coming of the Holy Spirit. At that time, Jesus would be available to believers in a different way than when He was here in the flesh. Believers would have a spiritual relationship with Him, not a physical relationship. In other words, the previous fellowship of sight, sound, and touch was ending, and His final state of glory was in process. The present was a gap between the period of the incarnation and His future glorious reign upon the throne of the universe. These in-between days with His followers were to be used for reassurance, consolation, preparation, and teaching; therefore, He had work to do, and He wanted Mary's help. That's why He discouraged her from clinging to Him. Instead He wanted her to go tell them what was happening.

APOSTLE TO THE APOSTLES

Mary did exactly as Jesus asked; she stopped clinging and started sharing. With conviction and certainty, she said to His disciples, "I have seen the Lord!" (John 20:18 NIV). What a change from the fear and puzzlement she felt on her earlier visit with them. Now, though, the mystery was solved. She had seen Jesus; He was alive!

She also told the disciples what Jesus said—how He was in the process of "returning" to His Father so He could eventually connect with all of His followers. His Father would be their Father, and His God would be their God. Jesus' Spirit, the Holy Spirit, would make this possible, but Jesus had to go away (He had to complete the process) for this to happen (see John 16:7).

Jesus was alive, and they could enjoy His presence for a time. But eventually He needed to be in glory where He would mediate for all of believers, making it possible for all people to experience Him spiritually. And sometimes those supernatural experiences are so grand that we want to cling to them just as Mary wanted to cling to the resurrected Jesus. As we ascend to new heights in our relationship with Jesus, when we have extraordinary spiritual experiences, we may want to keep the experience, hold on to it, and glorify it.

I remember once wanting to cling to a worship leader. Singing under Donald's leadership was meaningful, spiritual, and emotional, plus his life truly reflected Jesus. There was no manipulation of the audience or any performance in his leadership. In him, I saw Jesus. He just wanted to lead us in honoring and worshipping God. When we would be singing, sometimes I felt like I had died and gone to heaven. Never before had I wept in taking Communion, but I did when Donald had us worshipping through singing throughout the celebration. Thanksgiving for Jesus' sacrifice poured out of me. But church dynamics in which I was not involved strongly "encouraged" Donald to leave and move on to another church.

The Sunday night before his departure, we happened to be walking into church at the same time. I told him how much I hated to see him go and how much I appreciated his leadership. I shook his hand and said good-bye, but all I wanted to do was throw myself at his feet, hold on to him, and say, "Please, please don't go." Now that would not have been a pretty sight! But it was the way I felt. I wanted to keep my heaven on earth.

But Jesus said to me what He said to Mary Magdalene, "Don't cling. This is not the way it is in the Christian life. Instead, appreciate the experience, soak it up, relish it even, and then move on. Embrace what I have next for you. Remember you have a story to tell, one that says, 'I have seen Jesus.'"

FROM MIND TO HEART

How was Mary's response to the empty tomb different from Peter and John's?

Both the two angels and Jesus asked Mary, "Woman, why are you crying?" They surely knew why she was crying, so why might this question be important?

When has Jesus interrupted your tears or distress with a question? What did He ask? How did His question help?

What did Jesus say that caused Mary to recognize Him? Has He ever called you by name? How did this affect you?

What did Mary want to do when she realized Jesus was alive? Instead, what did Jesus tell her to do? Why?

How was Mary's news to the disciples the second time different from her first visit with them?

What is noteworthy about Mary's message, "I have seen the Lord"? Why should this be the testimony of every Christian?

PART V

WAS WHAT HE SPOKE
REALLY POSSIBLE?

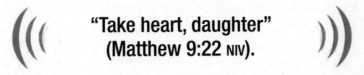

"Take heart, daughter" (Matthew 9:22 NIV).

RECENTLY I RAN INTO SOMEONE WHOM I HAD KNOWN YEARS EARLIER. Karen and I had lived in the same town for a while. We attended the same church before I moved away. As we caught up with each other, I asked her if she still went to that church.

She said, "No, I don't. I've moved on to another church several years ago."

"What church do you attend now?

She told me the name of the church, and I said, "Oh, I've heard the pastor preach; he's very impressive."

"Yes, he's a good preacher," Karen said. "He's really nice, but he's always trying to get me to join."

"You mean you haven't?" (Church membership is important in our denomination.)

"No, I haven't."

"Why not?"

"Oh, I couldn't do that. I couldn't stand in front of the church and say I want to be a member. I can't stand people looking at me."

I had to bite my lip to keep from saying, "Jesus died on the Cross for your sins so you could have a meaningful, purposeful life, and you don't have the courage to stand up in front of a group of people and say you want to join His church!"

As I walked away, I said to myself, "She could use some encouragement from another woman who didn't want to be seen."

WHAT WOMAN?

This woman who lived on the Capernaum side of the Sea of Galilee is not associated in the Bible with a location, a position or a name. Rather she is identified by her condition—the woman with an issue of blood. This is King James Version's way of describing continuous bleeding, and "issue" is a good way to describe it because the bleeding was a big issue in her life.

For 12 long years, continuous bleeding had dominated her existence. It made her work and everyday activities difficult. Constant attention had to be given to personal hygiene: frequent bathing, changing her clothing, and keeping her clothing clean. Nonstop attention was needed for nonstop bleeding.

The bleeding drained her physically and limited her socially. She felt weak most of the time. She had little interaction with others because she had to live mostly isolated from the rest of the community. Part of this was simply due to her wanting to avoid embarrassing incidents and maintaining personal hygiene, but the predominant reason was that she was unclean.

She wasn't unclean in the sense of being dirty like a child who has played in the mud, but she was unclean according to the Law of Moses,[1] the law the Jews lived by. The Law gave instructions to men for how to handle fluid discharge from the body such as semen and to women regarding menstrual flow both at regular times (during a menstrual period) and irregular times (bleeding in between periods or longer than usual). Here's some of what was involved.

- A woman could not attend a synagogue service while she was unclean.
- Other members of the community were not to touch bleeding women.
- No one could lie on the same bed as an unclean woman.
- No one could even sit on a chair that a bleeding woman had occupied.

- People could not touch any items that bleeding women might have handled.
- A woman could only become clean again after the bleeding stopped, and then a ritual bath must be taken to return to community activity.

In this woman's case, the bleeding didn't stop, so no ceremonial purification ever took place. This meant she had experienced years of avoiding people and being cut off from them. She didn't want to be around people, and they didn't want to be near her.

As a result, she had grown shy and reticent. While she didn't want any attention drawn to herself, she did want to be healed. In fact, she had put considerable effort in trying to be cured.

TWELVE LONG YEARS

From the time her bleeding became continuous, she started seeking a cure. Apparently, many remedies had been tried to no avail, and she "had suffered many things of many physicians" (Mark 5:26 KJV).

She "spent all she had on doctors, but no one had been able to cure her" (Luke 8:43). There was no change in her condition. Even though she depleted her finances, nothing was "bettered, but rather grew worse" (Mark 5:26 KJV). I can only imagine what the rest of her life would have been like if she hadn't heard about Jesus.

Did some person from a safe distance tell her about Him? Or did she hear stories about Him on rare visits to the market in Capernaum, a city in Galilee? Just as she made trips to see doctors, she must have gone to the open market to buy food. She had to eat, but few people probably volunteered to help her for fear of becoming unclean.

While she was careful not to talk to anyone and tried to make her purchases as quickly as possible, she still heard snippets about Jesus who performed miracles. How could she not when Galilee was where Jesus experienced His greatest popularity?

If I'm right about this possibility, it would explain why she fell in step with a crowd of people heading to the seashore. Their animated chatter allowed her to learn they were expecting Jesus to arrive. They talked about His recent miracle on the other side of the lake. He had cast out demons from a man and sent them into some swine. Some said, "What's He going to do next?" As she moved along with the crowd, she tried her best not to touch anyone, but she just had to follow! If Jesus were coming, if He really could perform miracles, then she wanted to see Him.

JESUS ARRIVED

As the crowd hurried toward the sea, more people joined them. It became harder and harder for the bleeding woman not to accidently bump them. Once Jesus arrived, and the multitudes gathered around Him, this became impossible.

The crowd, though, parted for Jairus, "an official in the local synagogue" (Luke 8:41). They made way for him because he was a person of authority, someone they knew and respected.

His presence added electricity to the gathering. Synagogue officials usually weren't receptive to Jesus. Knowing this made the spectators even more curious. Not only might they see a miracle, they might see some kind of argument or confrontation between Jesus and Jairus.

Jairus, though, wasn't interested in confronting Jesus. He was not there as a religious official but as a desperate father, concerned for his daughter, and he let it be known. He "threw himself down at Jesus' feet and begged him to go to his home, because his only daughter, who was twelve years old, was dying" (Luke 8:41–42).

Jesus agreed to go with Jairus to his home where his daughter was. As they went, the multitude "followed him, and thronged him" (Mark 5:24 KJV). They pressed and crushed against Him. Their radar was up as they wondered, *Could Jesus keep the girl from dying? Would the girl be healed? Would there be contention at Jairus's house?*

Whatever happened, they wanted to see! The crowd pushed, shoved, mingled, moved, and smashed up against one another as they made their way to Jairus's house. No one noticed the woman with the issue of blood, but she was noticing. She saw Jairus throw himself at Jesus' feet and beg Him for help. She was amazed at his boldness. She knew she could never ever do something like that. She could not go to Jesus in such a public way and make her affliction known. How embarrassing for her! How painful the glances and glares from the people would be! How angry they might be if they discovered an unclean person in their midst!

At the same time, she realized this might be her only chance to approach Jesus. From what she had heard, He never seemed to stay in one place very long. He might not be this way again, but how could she seek His help without risking a reaction from the crowd and possibly even from Jesus? Ceremonial law meant uncleanness for Him, too, if He touched her.

As she tried to think, something difficult to do while moving with the crowd, it occurred to her that if she could get close enough to touch His robe that might be connection enough for her to be healed. That way Jesus would never know an unclean person touched Him, and those in the thick crowd wouldn't know she had touched them. She could then be on her way, relieved and free of her scourge. The thought of being healed made her realize she must try although touching his garment would be a risky move. What if she bled more? What if her garment turned scarlet red? What if she were caught?

For a moment, she considered slipping out and going home, but no! This was her only chance! And she was going to take it!

 HER APPROACH

As she tried to make her way toward Jesus, the movement of the crowd worked against her, impeding her progress and making her feel guilty. She knew she was contaminating people, but it couldn't be helped if she was going to get to Jesus. She didn't want to defile people, but here was a chance for healing—a chance that might never come again. Jesus was a miracle worker, and a miracle is what she needed.

As fearfully and inconspicuously as possible, she maneuvered her way through the crowd to get behind Jesus where He wouldn't see her. That's when she was able to touch "the edge of his cloak" (Luke 8:44) and when she did, "her bleeding stopped at once." "She had the feeling inside herself that she was healed of her trouble" (Mark 5:29).

She could pull back now, work her way out of the crowd without anyone noticing, and get on with building a new life. She could have except Jesus startled her and everyone else. He stopped walking and asked, "Who touched me?" (Luke 8:45).

The disciples were incredulous. "You see how the people are crowding you; why do you ask who touched you?" (Mark 5:31).

"Peter said, 'Master, the people are all around you and crowding in on you'" (Luke 8:45). It would be impossible to know who touched Jesus in the dense, moving crowd. Others agreed and denied touching Him.

But Jesus knew someone had, someone who needed and received healing. He "kept looking around to see who had done it" (Mark 5:32). He said, "Someone touched me, for I knew it when power went out of me'" (Luke 8:46). (Every time Jesus healed someone, it cost Him something. This is one reason Jesus often needed retreats, time to be alone with God, so He could be replenished.)

The woman shivered as she heard this conversation. *Oh no, I didn't think Jesus would know. How could He know someone touched Him? What is going to happen now? Is He going to be angry that I've interrupted His urgent mission to Jairus's house? That I've defiled Him? That I've contaminated people in the crowd?*

Realizing she was going to be found out, she confessed. Trembling with fear, she threw herself at Jesus' feet, and told what she had done. "In front of everybody, she told him why she had touched him and how she had been healed at once" (v. 47). Then she held her breath, waiting to be chastised, but Jesus surprised her.

When Jesus turned around and saw her, He did not chide her for breaking the Law of Moses. He didn't criticize her for her actions. He didn't rebuke her for interrupting His journey, although I imagine this unexpected stop made Jairus want to rebuke her! Jesus didn't say, "We were on our way to help a dying child, and you're taking up valuable time." Instead, Jesus said, "Take heart, daughter . . . your faith has healed you" (Matthew 9:22 NIV).

WHAT JESUS SAID

This trembling, frightened woman needed comforting which is how the King James Version translates, "Take heart, daughter." Hers was a scary faith journey fraught with possibilities for ridicule and embarrassment, so while she was healed physically, she also needed spiritual healing. What better way to show her that He cared than by calling her "daughter." This is the only time in the gospels when Jesus addresses a woman as "daughter." In one word, Jesus let her know she was a cherished human being. Hearing this must have been a balm to her lonely heart.

Jesus not only wanted her to be comforted, He wanted to encourage her, hence the phrase "take heart." The heart that was fearful could now be strong because of what she had done. In other words, Jesus was saying, "Now do you realize you didn't have to be so reticent in approaching me? You are a braver woman than you gave yourself credit for being. Now use this newfound knowledge to embrace the life you have ahead of you." I like the way *The Message* expresses this, "Daughter, you took a risk in trusting me, and now you're healed and whole. Live well, live blessed!" (Luke 8:48). Now she could because she was a woman of faith.

Jesus said that her faith had healed her. Her faith, though, wasn't bold like Jairus's very public faith. It wasn't persistent like the

Syrophoenician woman's faith; if you remember, she refused to take no for answer. It wasn't daring like the street woman who publically crashed a dinner party to approach Jesus. So how could a woman who was trying to be discreet and not be found out have faith worthy of commendation?

Her faith moved her to take action; it moved her toward Jesus, the One who could help her. She chanced being embarrassed and possibly becoming an object of ridicule and anger to be healed. Her action, as inconspicuous as it was, said she had confidence and trust in Jesus. As a result, she was physically healed and spiritually renewed.

Jesus ended His comments to her with this directive, "Go in peace." She was free from all the inner turmoil she had experienced through the years. All the worry, the uncertainty, the hesitancy, and the fearfulness were gone. She was fully free to be herself, and this is why I wished Karen might "take heart" from her example.

BACK TO KAREN

Karen wasn't seeking physical healing like the woman with the issue of blood. I couldn't help but wonder, though, if there wasn't some part of her that needed healing. Why was it that she couldn't stand for people to look at her for the brief time it would take to join the church? She would not be facing a judgmental, critical group. Had something happened in her past that made her so self-conscious? Was there some unconfessed sin that made her feel unworthy or fear that she would be rejected?

Sometimes we have to risk being embarrassed just as the bleeding woman did if we want to be blessed. If Karen could move out from the pew and stand before the congregation—certainly an exercise of faith for her—she would receive church membership and more. She would experience the joy of proclaiming belief in Christ. She would gain a sense of family, feeling like she truly belonged. She would grow as an individual because she did something that frightened her, and she would gain the inner peace that comes with self-acceptance. She would be blessed.

The path of faith isn't always smooth or golden. Some discomfort may be involved in moving toward Jesus. Obstacles may stand in our way. Fear and apprehension may get a hold of us. Risk may be involved. We may have to take a chance on being embarrassed or even ridiculed. Or we may think our problem is too small, too insignificant considering the broad scheme of things. Or we could hold back because we think it is too big! We just don't have enough faith to believe Jesus would respond, but we shouldn't let these things get in the way. Jesus is saying to us, "Come, anyway. Don't let anything stand in your way. I've got time for you so take heart, daughter, and see what your faith will do."

FROM MIND TO HEART

On a scale of 1 to 10, with 10 being great faith, where would you place Jairus's faith? The woman's faith? On this same scale, where would you place your faith?

What causes some people to have strong faith and others to have weak faith?

How did Jesus know someone had touched Him? What does this tell you about Jesus?

What did Jesus say had made the woman well?

What are some problems that women might be reluctant to approach Jesus about?

What do you think Jesus meant when He said, "Take heart, daughter" (Matthew 9:22 NIV)? How can you "take heart" from Jesus' words to this daughter of His?

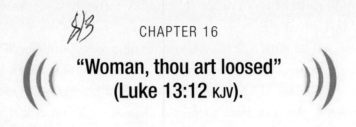

CHAPTER 16

"Woman, thou art loosed" (Luke 13:12 KJV).

IN THE EXERCISE CLASS I'M IN, THE INSTRUCTOR CONTINUALLY REMINDS us about our posture. She's always saying, "Pull those shoulders back"; "Hold in your tummy"; "Stand up straight"; etc. While we are not in the class because of our posture, her commands remind us that good posture is important to our health and well-being.

My mother—and sometimes an aunt or two—was always telling me to stand up straight when I was a teenager. Growing too fast, outpacing my classmates in height, and feeling awkward, I slumped. I don't know that these dear women were concerned with my health; they were concerned with my appearance. How I looked and how I carried myself would affect my relationships—especially getting a boyfriend!

Posture seems to be important to our health, to our appearance and to making connections. If this is true—and I believe it is—you can imagine how a woman with a severe posture problem must have been affected. She was bent over for 18 long years.

HER CONDITION

This nameless woman had "a spirit of infirmity" (Luke 13:11 KJV) which means she had an ailment of some kind that involved weakness, frailty, or feebleness. A wide range of things could cause this ailment, but whatever it was, it affected her posture. She "was bowed together, and could in no wise lift up herself."

Satan seems to have been responsible for her chronic and lengthy illness (see Luke 13:16), but this doesn't mean that she was demon possessed.[1] The devil himself through one of his evil spirits could have caused her infirmity, or she could have had arthritis, some spinal defect, an injury that never healed properly, or any of a number of things. The view in Jesus' day was that many maladies were caused by evil spirits. Regardless of whether her illness was caused by a physical ailment or an evil spirit, people would have said Satan caused it.

She had a hard time relating to people because of her curvature of the spine. Her eyes were directed toward the ground, so she couldn't look people in the eye. She couldn't see what others saw. She missed a lot of life because she couldn't look up.

She could, though, feel their stares as she shopped at the outdoor market and went to the synagogue. She knew she was being gawked at. Her deformity made her a pitiful sight which some people were uncomfortable with; even those people who were sympathetic found it too awkward to talk with her. They got so they just overlooked her.

Children, though, noticed her and talked with her. They were full of curious questions. What's wrong with you? How did this happen? Why can't you stand up straight? Can you straighten up at all?

The stares and the questions she could handle. Physically life was difficult. Because her spine was affected, she felt aches and pains throughout her body. Because she was bent over, her body was always in a rigid position. She could never really relax. What she wouldn't have given to be able to stretch out and lie flat for a good night's sleep, but she "could not straighten up at all" (Luke 13:11).

When the curvature first developed and before it became so rigid, she hoped for a cure, but the years since had taken their toll. After much mental and emotional distress, her hope turned to resignation.

She concluded, *What's the use of hoping? I'm always going to be like this.* Not only was her body broken, but her spirit was too.

Nevertheless, she had made a life for herself, even continuing to attend Sabbath services. She was "a daughter of Abraham" (13:16 NIV), a good Jewish woman, so she was there when the doors were open. That's why she was present the day Jesus visited her synagogue.

8|4   WHAT A CROWD

Many others were there too the day Jesus taught in the local Judean synagogue.

In addition to the bent-over woman, there were the regulars, those like her, the ones who were always there no matter what.

There were curious people; they had heard about some of the phenomenal things Jesus did, knew He was in town, and showed up just in case anything unusual happened. Maybe some healing would occur or perhaps some kind of confrontation might take place. Perhaps a Pharisee or two from Jerusalem might show up and challenge Jesus as they strongly opposed His teaching. Something interesting was bound to happen!

Some of Jesus' disciples were present too as He seldom traveled alone.

Then there was the synagogue official, the one keeping an eye on everything and who maintained the order of service.

Jews devoted to the law—both the written and oral law—were also in attendance. They wouldn't think of missing a Sabbath service.

The synagogue was filled with people, and Jesus taught them. As He looked around, He saw the bent-over woman. He noticed how serious her infirmity was. Why, the poor dear couldn't even raise her head. She could not fully straighten herself up to see Him, but *He saw her*.

The bent-over woman didn't approach Jesus. She didn't have a predetermined plan. It hadn't occurred to her that Jesus would want to help her. She couldn't even look pleadingly at Him, but the good news is, she didn't have to because in the synagogue, Jesus saw her.

WHAT SHE NEVER EXPECTED

Jesus saw this bent-over woman who had grown used to people not seeing her. He really looked at her, and He understood what kind of existence she had as a result of her condition. He responded by acting compassionately.

He called out to her. He didn't say to all of those in the synagogue, "If you're here today because you want to be healed, please come forward," or "I'll be glad to meet your needs once the service is over." Instead, He signaled her out as if she were the only person in the room and called to her.

He spoke to her. This woman who was used to people not talking to her was addressed by the Teacher in their midst. This surprised her, but what was even more surprising is what He said.

He said to her as she moved toward Him, "Woman, thou art loosed from thine infirmity" (Luke 13:12 KJV). According to Herbert Lockyer, "Thou art loosed" is a phrase medical writers used "to describe release from disease, relaxing tensions, and taking off of bandages."[2] This woman was indeed being loosed from the tension, the bondage, the discomfort, and the embarrassment that had tied her up for so long. She never expected to hear freeing words like this, and they were spoken to her even before she reached Jesus.

He touched her. When she reached Him, Jesus laid His hands upon her. She felt an indescribable power move through her body. As it moved, she could feel her spine start to unwind. "Immediately she was made straight" (v. 13 KJV). After 18 long years of physical deformity, contracted muscles relaxed, the spine's curvature vanished, and she could stand erect. Satan had bound this woman, tying her up in a bent position, holding her back, keeping her from being all she could be, and now the binding was gone.

On a day when she hadn't been expecting help, Jesus set her free from Satan's grip, and she didn't even have to ask Him. Jesus took the initiative, and unsolicited, uttered words of healing.

What Jesus said to this woman, He wants to say to those of us today who are bent over in some way and who can't seem to straighten up. What are some of those things that might make women feel bound or bent over?

BENT-OVER WOMEN

Many of us have or will have infirmities at some time or another as we move through life.

We may be bent over by obligations. You may be so overburdened with responsibilities and relationship demands that you feel like you're carrying the weight of the world on your shoulders. People see the tension in the way you hold yourself. They often ask, "Are you all right?"

We may be bent over by grief. A loss may be so great that you don't feel like looking up anymore. You identify with the psalmist who said, "I am troubled; I am *bowed down greatly*; I go mourning all the day long" (Psalm 38:6 KJV; author's italics).

We may be bent over by aging. Your body tilts forward or you develop a dowager's hump. You hate this because you're aware of the ageism prevalent in our society. Even though you feel young, you're aware that some people typecast you as being hopelessly out of date.

We may be crippled by severe physical pain. Back pain is one of the most common physical ailments in the United States, and if you have it, you can't help but carry yourself in a rigid way. Otherwise the pain is just too intense to manage.

Paul suffered pain that laid Him low from time to time. It is described in his second letter to the Corinthians as one of his "infirmities" (2 Corinthians 12:5 KJV). He referred to this pain as a "thorn in the flesh" (v. 7 KJV) and as coming from Satan just as the bent-over woman's infirmity was.

We may be depressed. A person's depression may be reflected in the way she holds herself. I said to a young adult recently, "The way you hold your head and the position of your shoulders reflect sadness. Are you depressed?" She said she wasn't, but her eyes said she was. I wondered if she had been this way for so long that being sad seemed normal, and it affected her physical being without her being aware of it.

These are some possibilities—far from a complete list—of some of the things that can get us bent out of shape, but take heart, sisters. Jesus can help us with our infirmities, enabling us to stand straight.

5 JESUS' NATURE

The Bible shows over and over again that Jesus responds to infirmities.

When speaking of Jesus as the Servant of God, Isaiah said, "He took up our pain and bore our suffering" (Isaiah 53:4 NIV).

Isaiah also said Jesus would "bind up the brokenhearted"; "proclaim liberty to the captives"; and open "the prison" of "them that are bound" (61:1 KJV). He said Jesus would make "crooked things straight" (42:16 KJV).

A psalmist said, "The LORD raiseth them that are bowed down" (Psalm 146:8 KJV).

Matthew said that Jesus "cast out the spirits with his word, and healed all that were sick" (Matthew 8:16 KJV) and took "our infirmities" upon "Himself" and bore "our sicknesses" (v. 17 KJV).

Luke wrote that after Jesus healed a man with a serious case of leprosy, "great multitudes came together to hear, and to be healed by him of their infirmities" (Luke 5:15 KJV).

To confirm for John the Baptist that Jesus was indeed the Anointed One sent from God, Jesus "cured many of their infirmities and plagues, and of evil spirits" (7:21 KJV). His works were confirmed that He was sent from God.

Jesus healed the Galilean women who supported His ministry of "evil spirits and infirmities" (8:2 KJV). How I wish I could hear their stories! I wonder what Jesus said to them.

He healed a man who had been sick for 38 years of his infirmity by the pool in Jerusalem (see John 5:1–9). And in this chapter, we have seen where Jesus healed the bent-over woman of hers.

That Jesus sees, understands, and straightens infirmities, doesn't mean He always straightens in the same way every time. No routine was followed every time. Jesus did not have a canned method for healing or a "works every time" formula.

With the bent-over woman, He saw, He called, He spoke, and He touched.

With the man by the pool, the one who had an infirmity for 38 years, He started with a question, "Do you want to get well?" (John 5:6). He ended with a command for action. Jesus said, "Get up, pick up your mat, and walk" (v. 8).

With Paul and his infirmity, Jesus said, "My grace is sufficient for thee" (2 Corinthians 12:9 KJV). Paul could straighten up and continue serving God because He was given sufficient grace.

Jesus' Spirit also helps with "our infirmities" (Romans 8:26 KJV). The Holy Spirit "maketh intercession for us with groanings which cannot be uttered."

Jesus may see us and call out our healing. One day, to our surprise, we experience a relaxation of the tension that has been affecting our posture.

Or we may need to approach Him, to show ourselves as open and eager for Him to work in our lives.

Either way, here's what we can count on: Jesus is "touched with the feeling of our infirmities" (Hebrews 4:15 KJV), and in Him, we "obtain mercy, and find grace to help in time of need" (v. 16 KJV).

When the breakthrough comes, no matter how it might occur, whether through our initiative or His, there may be someone who wants to throw a damper on our newfound freedom just as someone did when the bent-over woman was straightened.

8) 6 THERE'S ALWAYS ONE

You can imagine how grateful and relieved the bent-over woman was when Jesus freed her. The woman "praised God" (Luke 13:13). She was a happy woman; however, someone who observed the miracle was less than joyful. He wasn't an evil man; rather he was someone very religious who earnestly wanted to see rules and rituals followed. He was the ruler of the synagogue.

Rather than rejoicing over this woman's good fortune, all the ruler could see was Jesus breaking the Sabbath rules. The ruler was indignant! How dare Jesus heal someone on the Sabbath! Healing was work, and you didn't work on the Sabbath! So angry was the official that he had to speak. He couldn't keep quiet.

He didn't address Jesus directly. Perhaps this was because Jesus was a guest at the synagogue or because he wasn't sure how Jesus might react. Rather the ruler addressed the synagogue attendees, as if he were teaching them. He said, "There are six days in which we should work; so come during those days and be healed, but not on the Sabbath!" (v. 14).

Actually, Jesus could have helped the bent-over woman the next day. When He saw her, He could have called her aside, and said, "Come back tomorrow when the Sabbath is over, and I will free you of your infirmity." She had lived for 18 years this way; another day was not going to matter, but He didn't and He said why.

There were others in attendance who felt the same way as the synagogue official. Jesus addressed them all.

"You hypocrites," He said, and then He reminded them of something they did on the Sabbath. They loosed their animals from their stalls and watered them. That was perfectly legal so surely it was right in the sight of God to loose a poor woman from her infirmity. Why should she needlessly have to suffer another day? A woman is more important than an ox, her bondage by an evil spirit more important than an ox's bondage by a rope, particularly since she was a daughter of Abraham.

Jesus' reasoning put His adversaries to shame and silenced them. They said no more.

The people, as a whole, were amazed; they rejoiced over Jesus' actions and His words. And that's the camp I want to be in, don't you? I want to be a part of the group that recognizes the power of Jesus. That's when I want to throw my shoulders back, stand up straight, and glorify God!

FROM MIND TO HEART

What does this incident and Jesus' response tell us about His nature?

What are some crooked things that might need to be made straight in our lives?

How is this woman's encounter with Jesus like that of the Nain widow's?

Because Jesus saw the bent-over woman's need, does this mean we should never take the initiative in seeking His healing? Should we wait for Him to see us?

What makes you uptight and rigid?

What does your posture, your countenance, or the way you carry yourself say about you?

What might cause a person to be more concerned with religious rules than with spiritual healing?

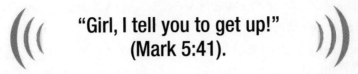

CHAPTER 17

"Girl, I tell you to get up!"
(Mark 5:41).

WHAT ONE WORD WOULD YOU USE TO DESCRIBE YOUR FATHER? I WOULD use *rescuer*. Numerous times he had to come to my aid, particularly when I was trying to become an independent adult and make a life for myself.

In college, home for Christmas break, I awoke in the middle of the night with excruciating pain. While Mom wrung her hands, Dad scooped me up and took me to the hospital.

In my first year teaching in Chicago, I had an automobile accident, and surgery followed. Dad drove five hours in 14-degree-below weather to get me and take me home.

In my second year of teaching, when I had a serious case of the flu and was too weak to take care for myself, Dad arrived. He helped me to his car, took me home, and called the doctor.

When I think about times like these, I am reminded of Jairus (whom we encountered in chap. 15), another father who was also in the rescue business. His daughter's situation, though, was a lot more severe than mine.

SHE WAS DYING

Jairus's daughter was on the brink of womanhood. She was 12 years old. A Jewish girl became a woman at the age of 12 years and one day. Life was opening up before her, and her future was bright. She would mature, get married, leave home, have children, and live a life that her parents would take pride in. Their dreams and hopes for her, though, were being threatened. Something was dreadfully wrong with their daughter. She was "very sick" (Mark 5:23). In fact, she was "at the point of death" (KJV).

Jairus, of course, had taken her to doctors in the area, but they were stumped by her symptoms and offered no help or encouragement. He wasn't used to being in such a helpless position. As a ruler of the local synagogue, Jairus was a strong man and an authoritative leader. He was a problem solver, and yet this illness of his daughter's was appearing to be one he couldn't solve. She was getting weaker and weaker.

As Jairus watched her condition deteriorate, he decided, "I've got to do something. I can't just stand by and watch her die." As he pondered what to do, the name Jesus flashed before him. He had heard stories of Jesus doing very unusual things. Some of his colleagues had approached Jesus on behalf of a Roman centurion whose servant was near death; the servant was healed (see Luke 7:1–10)! There was talk around town about Jesus' having brought a widow's dead son back to life.[1] Should he go to Jesus? He hesitated. What would his professional colleagues think? While some like those few who witnessed the centurion servant's healing appreciated Jesus, many despised Him.

THE JEWS REACTION TO JESUS

Jairus was part of an elite group of Jewish men. They were the rulers or officials of the synagogues. They were knowledgeable men who were responsible for the correct administration of the synagogue including its services and finances. The rulers of the synagogue, elected by people in the community, were well respected and very influential.

The reason these esteemed leaders disliked Jesus was because He went against the oral law that they defended. One thing Jesus did that particularly irritated them was breaking the Sabbath rules as outlined in the oral law (the Traditions of the Elders). Consequently, they branded Jesus as a heretic and a sinner. So tight was the organization of rulers that any man in Jairus's position would feel the force of their official ire if he identified himself with Jesus in any way. They expected Jairus to stay away from Jesus, but Jairus was having second thoughts. Some of the stories about what Jesus had done called to him, "Here's help. Here's hope."

Any other time Jairus might have deliberated long about risking the disapproval of his colleagues. He would have talked with other synagogue leaders and considered the repercussions, but time was crucial. His precious daughter wasn't getting better, and he needed help. If Jesus was his only hope, then he was going to pursue Him.

SEEKING HELP

Jairus found Jesus on the Capernaum side of the Sea of Galilee. A large crowd clustered around Jesus, but the people parted slightly when they saw Jairus. Taking advantage of this space, he moved closer to Jesus. Recognizing He was in the presence of hope, Jairus forgot about his dignity, his colleagues, and the people watching. "He threw himself down at [Jesus'] feet and begged him earnestly, 'My little daughter is very sick. Please come and place your hands on her, so that she will get well and live!'" (Mark 5:22–23).

Jesus tenderly knelt beside the prostrate father[2] and spoke words of comfort to Jairus. Then "Jesus got up and followed him, and his disciples went along with him" (Matthew 9:19). Naturally the already curious multitude followed, with people "crowding him from every side" (Mark 5:24). This was frustrating for Jairus because the crowd slowed their pace. They could have moved much faster without them. As if the tight crowd wasn't enough frustration, something else happened to slow them down.

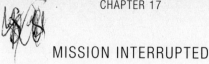

MISSION INTERRUPTED

Jesus stopped to help a woman with a severe bleeding problem (see chap. 15). Any other day Jairus would have been sympathetic, but now every minute counted. If Jesus could just get to his house, lay hands on his daughter, then she might recover. The slow progress of the crowd made him impatient; stopping for this woman made him frantic. Outwardly Jairus appeared calm, but inwardly he was fuming. Every wasted minute threatened his daughter's life. Jesus didn't see it that way. Jesus had time for both the bleeding woman and Jairus's daughter.

While Jesus was helping the woman, messengers from Jairus's home arrived. They said to him, "Your daughter has died. Why bother the Teacher any longer?" (Mark 5:35).

At these words, Jairus felt his energy drain from his body. It was all he could do to hold himself upright as he realized his effort to save his daughter had been in vain.

While Jairus was affected by the messengers' words, Jesus was not. He "paid no attention to what they said" (v. 36). Jesus said to Jairus, "Don't be afraid, only believe."

Jesus insisted they go on, and He dispatched the crowd. "He did not let anyone else go on with him except Peter and James and his brother John" (v. 37).

When the men arrived at Jairus's home, the death wailing had already begun, telling all the tragic news. Mourners filled the air with laments and cries of bereavement. Family, friends, and possibly professional mourners beat their breasts, tore their garments, and pulled their hair. This made for a noisy and confusing environment.

Mark talks about their making much ado and weeping (v. 38).

Luke says "all wept, and bewailed her" (8:52 KJV).

Matthew says Jesus "saw the minstrels and the people making a noise" (9:23 KJV). Flute players with their shrill, sad melodies were an integral part of mourning in most homes.

When Jesus saw the musicians and how stirred up the people were, "He said, 'Get out, everybody! The little girl is not dead—she is only sleeping!'" (vv. 23–24).

His statement was too much! She wasn't sleeping! The girl was dead! They all knew that, and they "started making fun of him." The King James Version says, "They laughed him to scorn" (Mark 5:40).

All evidence indicated the girl was dead, and there was nothing anyone could do, but the mourners didn't know Jesus. In the face of evidence that screamed "impossible," Jesus said "possible." Jesus can see hope and possibilities where others cannot, and this is something we need to keep in mind as we look for solutions in our own lives. Our vision is always limited but Jesus has the wider view as He did in this case. He saw a future for a girl who was declared dead. Hence, in His eyes, she was indeed only sleeping.

 ## RAISING HER UP

Jesus put everyone out of the house except for the parents and Peter, James, and John. This was no place for gawkers, doubters, or hecklers.

"Jesus went into the girl's room and took hold of her hand" (Matthew 9:25). With that gesture, warmth entered her cold body and her resuscitation begun.

Jesus said to her, "*Talitha, koum*" (Mark 5:41). Don't recognize those words? That's because they are Aramaic, the "at home" language of the Jews. While the New Testament was written in Greek, the language of the marketplace, some Aramaic phrases were kept and preserved. Two other examples include the healing of a deaf mute when Jesus said, "'*Ephphatha*' which means 'Open up!'" (7:34) and Jesus' cry from the Cross, "'*Eloi, Eloi, lema sabachthani*,' which means 'My God, my God, why did you abandon me?'" (15:34).

These Aramaic words were probably kept because they were indelibly printed on the hearts of the eyewitnesses. Some experiences are just so wonderful, so dramatic, so emotional, or so unusual that you always remember particular details such as specific words. And then when you talk about the experience, you repeat the words just as they were said. To tell it any other way would take away from the marvel of the experience.

When Peter, James, or John told the Gospel writer Mark of this impressive incident, they couldn't help but repeat Jesus' powerful Aramaic words, "*Talitha, koum.*" In English, this means "Child! Arise!" The Good News Translation translates the words this way: "Little girl, I tell you to get up!" (5:41).

In response to Jesus' strong command, the girl "got up at once" (Luke 8:55) and "her life returned." She "started walking around" (Mark 5:42). When this happened, those in the room "were completely amazed." I love the way the King James Version describes their reaction. It says "they were astonished with a great astonishment" (KJV). Death is so irrevocable. The reality of it was right before them, and Jesus revoked death! The girl came alive right before their eyes. Wow! This is astonishing!

Then Jesus did a couple of things that I would call odd if anyone else did them.

1. Jesus said, "Give her something to eat" (v. 43). The Bible commentators I read said Jesus did this to prove that she was healed, that she truly was alive. I don't agree. If she got up as Jesus commanded—which she did—and walked around, then clearly she was raised from the dead. What more proof would have been needed?

   I wonder if the explanation could be something as simple as a preventative measure for her future. Perhaps she had been unable to eat as part of her sickness or perhaps not eating caused her illness, and now that she was healed, it was important that she began to rebuild her health. Jesus was concerned about her future as well as the present.

2. "Jesus commanded them not to tell anyone what had happened"

(Luke 8:56). If you were experiencing a moment like this—one of being "astonished with a great astonishment" over a loved one's being rescued from death—wouldn't you want to tell someone? Wouldn't that be the natural response? Yet Jesus told this family not to tell. In fact, He "gave them strict orders not to tell anyone" (Mark 5:43).

This miracle was one you would want to retell again and again because a girl declared dead was declared alive. Scholars give various reasons for Jesus' commanding them not to tell.

- Jesus needed to protect His messianic mission. There was much work and training to do before it was time to reveal that He was the Messiah. Too much talk about His miracles might force a premature announcement.

- His miracles of healing were done primarily out of compassion rather than out of a desire to demonstrate His power to unbelievers. To broadcast His phenomenal action would exacerbate the huge superficial following He was already experiencing. He wanted true followship where people would follow His teachings.

- Jesus didn't want to set a precedent that would make people bring every dying person back to life or heal every sick person that came to Him for help. Each mighty act brought more people clamoring for His help, but His mission was about more than healing.

I don't know what the reason was, but I do know this: I would have had to tell! I could not have witnessed a super miracle like the healing of Jairus's daughter and kept quiet. Those there the day Jairus's daughter was resurrected surely felt the same way because "the news about this spread all over that part of the country" (Matthew 9:26). Someone had to have told! I'm glad they did. I'm glad the story has been told and retold so those of us whose spirit languishes at times can be encouraged to take Jesus' hand and listen for Him to say, "Girl, I tell you to get up."

REVIVING THE SPIRIT

Interestingly, of Jairus's daughter's healing, the King James Version says, "Her spirit came again" (Luke 8:55). The Revised Standard Version says, "Her spirit returned." We sometimes find ourselves in situations where our human spirit feels as if it has died or is dying. It hasn't really but it can become limp or dormant. When I described those times my father rescued me, I described the physical symptoms—excruciating pain, surgery, the flu—and yet behind them was a languishing spirit—a spirit that needed healing.

When the excruciating pain occurred in the middle of the night while I was home for Christmas break, I was also dealing with the weariness of serving the Lord. Yes, you read that right. Sometimes we can become weary in well doing, and I was from dealing with the dynamics and politics of leadership in a religious organization.

In my first year teaching in Chicago, when I had the accident and subsequent surgery, I was consciously living outside of the will of God. As I mentioned in chapter 9, I made the decision to work in Chicago without even asking God where He wanted me to work. It turned out not to be a good fit for me, and I was miserable.

When I had the flu and couldn't care for myself, I was weak from trying—really "overtrying"—to be a good teacher and from trying to make a life for myself. Although I was much older than Jairus's daughter, I was on the brink of womanhood like she was, and was beginning to wonder if I was ever going to find myself and my place in the world.

Recovery from each of these things gave me time to think and the quiet necessary for listening. I had the time to evaluate my life, my motives, and my relationship with God. More importantly, in the quiet of my parents' home, when I wearied of watching television, I was forced to listen. I eventually heard Jesus say, "Girl, it's time to get up and to get going." It took a while. In the case of the Chicago incident, it took months, but the point is that I did hear Him, and when I *got up*, I found my spirit had returned.

When reality gets us down, when all around the evidence looks as hopeless as Jairus's daughter's condition looked to the messengers, then it's time to take hold of Jesus' hand and listen for Him to say, "Girl, get up." When we do, when we take action, our vision improves, our spirit is renewed, and we feel fully alive.

FROM MIND TO HEART

Why might Jesus have put the crowd outside to heal Jairus's daughter when He healed the woman with the issue of blood with people all around Him?

What are some times in a woman's life when her spirit may be dormant?

When might Jesus want to say "get up" to a woman?

Was Jairus's approaching Jesus for help an act of faith or desperation?

Once the messengers arrived, Jesus did not allow any of the crowd to continue on with Him and Jairus except Peter, James, and John. Why did Jesus do this?

Other than gaining quiet, why did Jesus put everyone out of the room?

Why did Jesus include Peter, James, and John in the girl's room? You could certainly understand His including the parents, but why these three men?

PART VI
THE FULFILLING WORD

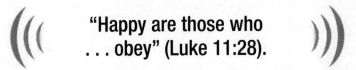

CHAPTER 18

"Happy are those who . . . obey" (Luke 11:28).

MAYBE YOU'VE BEEN AT A HIGH SCHOOL GRADUATION AND HEARD A mother way up in the bleachers yell, "That's my boy!" when her son received his diploma.

Maybe you've been to a football game when a touchdown is scored. Amid the cheers, you hear someone say, "Did you see that? That's my kid!"

If you have, then you can easily picture a scene in Jesus' life when a woman was so impressed by His teaching that she had to express herself. Her words, though, weren't about Him; they were about His mother.

"When Jesus had said this . . ."

How long the woman had been following and listening to Jesus is hard to tell, but she was definitely present the day Jesus drove a demon out of a man who couldn't talk. She, along with the crowd, was amazed.

Some in the crowd connected Jesus' power to do this with Beelzebul, the chief of demons.

"Others wanted to trap Jesus, so they asked him to perform a miracle to show that God approved of him" (Luke 11:16).

Jesus responded to them in two ways: (1) if what He was doing was attributed to Beelzebul, then this meant their own exorcists were too; and (2) if the prince of demons was lending his power to defeat his own emissaries, then Beelzebul was finished.

CHAPTER 18

"Happy are those who . . . obey" (Luke 11:28).

MAYBE YOU'VE BEEN AT A HIGH SCHOOL GRADUATION AND HEARD A mother way up in the bleachers yell, "That's my boy!" when her son received his diploma.

Maybe you've been to a football game when a touchdown is scored. Amid the cheers, you hear someone say, "Did you see that? That's my kid!"

If you have, then you can easily picture a scene in Jesus' life when a woman was so impressed by His teaching that she had to express herself. Her words, though, weren't about Him; they were about His mother.

"When Jesus had said this . . ."

How long the woman had been following and listening to Jesus is hard to tell, but she was definitely present the day Jesus drove a demon out of a man who couldn't talk. She, along with the crowd, was amazed.

Some in the crowd connected Jesus' power to do this with Beelzebul, the chief of demons.

"Others wanted to trap Jesus, so they asked him to perform a miracle to show that God approved of him" (Luke 11:16).

Jesus responded to them in two ways: (1) if what He was doing was attributed to Beelzebul, then this meant their own exorcists were too; and (2) if the prince of demons was lending his power to defeat his own emissaries, then Beelzebul was finished.

181

Jesus insisted that it was "by means of God's power that" He drove "out demons," proving "that the Kingdom of God" had come to them (v. 20). I'm sure the woman's mouth was gaping open about now, and she was thinking, *Brilliant answer!*

Jesus let the people know that their standoffishness was really working against God. "Anyone who is not for me is really against me; anyone who does not help me gather is really scattering" (v. 23). She thought to herself, *That's right. We should all work together.*

She was further fascinated when Jesus told about an evil spirit going out of a person, looking for a place to land, and then goes back to the person and brings other spirits with him. This story explained a lot of what she had observed in life.

As she listened, she marveled at Jesus' mental acuity, His wisdom, His authority, and the way He answered His critics. What a mind! What insight! She thought of His mother. She must feel so proud and so honored to have raised such a son. The woman couldn't help but express herself. She raised her voice and said, "How happy is the woman who bore you and nursed you!" (v. 27).

Her view of happiness was probably shared by many in the crowd. Bearing children, as noted earlier in this book, was considered the highest privilege of womanhood. Imagine, then, how startled she must have been when Jesus defined happiness another way.

JESUS' DEFINITION

Jesus said, "Rather, how happy are those who hear the word of God and obey it!" (Luke 11:28). The King James Version and the New International Version use the word "blessed" instead of "happy." The Greek word which is translated as "happy" and "blessed" is *makarios*, a word that refers to inner happiness. It means feeling fortunate and well off not materially but spiritually.

Jesus' definition did not negate what the woman said as some Bible versions make clear.

- "But He said, Yea, rather, blessed are they that hear the word of God, and keep it" (KJV).
- "But He said, 'Yes, but better still, blessed are those who listen to God's message and practice it!'" (Williams).
- "He replied, 'Yes, but even more blessed are all who hear the Word of God and put it into practice'" (TLB).

Motherhood and having children you can be proud of is a blessed state, but not everyone can be a mother or wants to be a mother. Neither does every mother have children that turn out well so only a limited number could be blessed. Jesus widened the range of who could be blessed, and at the same time, revealed what He considered of prime importance. In His eyes, what's important is hearing and keeping the word of God—something that's possible for males and females, married or single, old and young, rich and poor, parents and children, whatever their color, and whatever their race.

BLESSED ARE THE HEARERS

The hearing that Jesus speaks of doesn't mean having the right volume. Many in Jesus' audience heard the words Jesus spoke in the sense that He was loud enough, but they weren't blessed because their lives remained unchanged. The words never penetrated. The "hearing" that leads to being blessed means taking in, grasping, and absorbing.

This is the kind of hearing we've aimed for in this book as we listened in on conversations Jesus had with women. We looked at the context—where Jesus was in His life and where the women were. We considered cultural elements and word meanings. We amplified what He said so we could really hear—so His words would penetrate.

- We heard Him say some things that had a shock element to them. His words made us want to ask, "How's that again?"
- We heard Him speak to and forgive sinful women—an adulterer and a prostitute, recalling for us the wonder of forgiveness.

- We heard Him talk about Himself, giving us insight into His nature—He is Living Water, He is sent from God, and He is the resurrection and the life.
- We also heard Him console women and were comforted to know that He will "be there" for us when we need Him.
- We listened as He spoke encouraging words to women who needed wholeness and healing—words such as "Take heart," "Thou art loosed," and "I tell you to get up!"

Hearing, as important as it is, though, is not enough according to Jesus to have a blessed or happy life. It requires something more. It requires obedience.

BLESSED ARE THE KEEPERS

If someone asked you how to be happy, would you suggest being obedient? I doubt that I would because I don't usually associate obedience with happiness. I am more likely to link obedience with hard work, discipline, and self-denial, and yet Jesus connected it with happiness. In other words, some effort is required if we want to be blessed. This is evident in some of the instructions He gave to the women He helped.

- To the Samaritan woman at the well, Jesus said, "*Go*, call thy husband, and come hither" (John 4:16 KJV, author's emphasis).
- To the woman caught in adultery, Jesus said, "*Go*, and sin no more" (8:11 KJV, author's emphasis).
- To Mary Magdalene at the tomb, Jesus said, "*Go* to my brethren" (20:17 KJV, author's emphasis).
- To the woman who washed His feet and to the woman with the issue of blood, He said, "*Go* in peace (Luke 7:50; Mark 5:34 KJV, author's emphasis).
- To Jairus's daughter, whom Jesus resurrected, He said, "Girl, I tell you to *get up!*" (Mark 5:41, author's emphasis).

Even when specific instructions weren't given, follow through was needed *if* the woman wanted to be blessed. If you hear the words *You are forgiven* and you do not act as if you are, the words will not contribute to your inner happiness. If you say, "Yes, I can drink the cup of suffering," but do not follow Jesus when rough times occur, you will not feel blessed. To have the quality of *makarios* doesn't mean having a perfect life. It is not one where you get everything you want. Neither does it mean having everything under control although these things could be considered blessings. *Makarios* is about an inner, spiritual quality promised to those who hear and obey. It is not dependent on circumstances, as these comments from some Christian women reflect.

- An international missionary says, "Don't feel sorry for me" when you say, "I don't see how you live in such trying circumstances."
- When you say to a foster parent who has had numerous children going in and out of her life, "I couldn't do what you do," she smiles. Her eyes light up as she speaks, "It's my joy to 'be there' for these children during troubling transitions in their lives."
- A widow remarks, "My aloneness has given me opportunities to serve God in ways I never thought possible."
- A mother of adult children who have disappointed her maintains, "The well of Living Water still bubbles up because Jesus is the resurrection and the life. I believe things will get better."

When we hear and obey, we have sense of purpose, and we are at peace with ourselves and with God. We have the sense that Jesus is with us, that His Spirit guides us, and affirms His realness. We feel fully alive.

GETTING PERSONAL

In this book, we've heard what Jesus said to women and considered what His words might mean for us today. Now it's time to decide what we are going to do with what He said. Shall we let what we have learned spill over into our lives and affect how we live?

In each chapter, I tried to make an application of what Jesus' words mean to women today by sharing what He said to me. What He said to you may differ from what He said to me, but what's important for both of us is our response. Are we going to be keepers of His Word? Are we going to obey? I plan to, and keep in mind that I said I think obedience is hard! I know it won't be easy. I know I will fail at times, but when I do, I will pick myself up and continue working at being obedient because I've been amazed by Jesus. I've heard Him say things like, "Take heart"; "Your sins are forgiven"; and "I am the resurrection and the life."

What will you do with what Jesus said to you? Why don't you join me and be a hearer and keeper of the Word? You'll be amazed at what you hear and experience. That's when you will want to exclaim as I've been exclaiming, "Guess what He said to me!"

Notes

CHAPTER 4

1. Some of the Galilean women are named in Luke 8:1–3. Salome is not named there, but she is named as a part of this group in Mark 15:40–41 and Mark 16:1.

2. For this chapter, we're following the account in Matthew where she speaks to Jesus on behalf of a position for her sons. Another Gospel shows James and John asking Jesus (Mark 10:35–45).

3. Matthew 16:21; 17:22–23; and 20:17–19.

4. Matthew 27:56; Mark 15:40–41.

CHAPTER 5

1. See John 6:14–15.

2. See Mark 1:23–27.

3. William Barclay, *The Gospel of Matthew,* vol. 2, *The Daily Study Bible* (Edinburgh, Scotland: The Saint Andrew Press, 6th imprint, 1965), 135.

4. Dwight Moody, T. De Witt Talmage, and Joseph Parker, *Bible Characters* (Chicago: Thos. W. Jackson Publishing Company, 1902), 265.

5. See Romans 8:26–27.

6. See Hebrews 11:6.

CHAPTER 6

1. Ray Summers, *Commentary on Luke* (Waco, TX: Word Books, 1972), 302.

2. Until modern-day Israel.

CHAPTER 7

1. See Deuteronomy 22:22–23.

2. I learned this form of praying from Rosalind Rinker, *Communicating Love Through Prayer* (Grand Rapids, MI: Zondervan Publishing House, 1966), 105.

CHAPTER 8

1. William Barclay, *The Gospel of Luke, The Daily Study Bible,* 3rd ed. (Edinburgh, Scotland: The Saint Andrew Press, 1964), 94.

2. From the old hymn "I Stand Amazed in the Presence" by Charles H. Gabriel.

CHAPTER 9

1. See Genesis 1:27

2. See John 7:37–39a.

3. Christin Ditchfield, blog, May 30, 2013.

4. R. A. Torrey, "A Source of Joy Ever Springing Up," Decision magazine, May 1999, 33.

CHAPTER 11

1. John 11:5.

2. Luke 10:38–42.

3. In this chapter that focuses on what Jesus said to Martha, there's not room to explore why Jesus might have delayed returning to Bethany. For insight as to why He didn't go back immediately, see chapter 14 in my book *Reaching Heaven: Discovering the Cornerstones of Jesus' Prayer Life.*

4. William Barclay, *The Gospel of John,* vol. 2, *The Daily Study Bible,* 3rd ed. (Edinburgh, Scotland: The Saint Andrew Press, 1964), 119.

5. Ibid., slightly rephrased by author.

6. Brenda Poinsett, *Understanding a Woman's Depression* (Wheaton, IL: Tyndale House Publishers Inc., 1984), 173–74.

7. John 10:10.

CHAPTER 12

1. William Barclay*, And He Had Compassion: The Healing Miracles of Jesus* (Valley Forge: Judson Press, 1975), 116.

2. Later in the story, after the miracle, the people see him as a prophet, but nothing indicates they saw Jesus as the Son of God with divine authority.

3. See Numbers 19:11.

4. Chronologically, this was the first manifestation of Jesus' power to raise the dead.

5. See 2 Kings 4:8–37.

6. See 1 Kings 17:8–24.

7. Also known as Abram.

8. Also known as Sarai.

9. See Isaiah 66:13.

CHAPTER 13

1. This incident is also recorded in Matthew 13:48–50 and Luke 8:19–21.

2. To learn more about these women—and to see them as a group—you might want to study these Bible passages: Luke 8:1–3; 23:49, 55–56; 24:10; Mark 15:40–41; Matthew 27:55–56; and John 19:25–27

3. The Interpreter's Bible, vol. 8 (Nashville: Abingdon Press, 1955), 782.

CHAPTER 14

1. Rabboni is simply an Aramaic form of rabbi; she recognized her teacher and master.

2. R. V. G. Tasker, *The Gospel According to St. John,* Tyndale Bible Commentaries, New Testament Series, vol. 4 (Grand Rapids, MI: Wm. B. Eerdmans Publishing Company, 1965), 225.

CHAPTER 15

1. See Leviticus 15:19–33.

CHAPTER 16

1. Nothing about this incident or her subsequent healing, as we shall see, indicates demon possession. This incident in Luke 13:10–17 describes a healing rather than an exorcism.

2. Herbert Lockyer, All the Women of the Bible (Grand Rapids, MI: Zondervan Publishing House, 1988), 234.

CHAPTER 17

1. Harmony of the gospels puts this incident before this one with Jairus's daughter.

2. That Jesus had knelt is implied in Matthew 9:19a.

Acknowledgments

In researching for my book *Wonder Women of the Bible*, I read that Jesus made some of His most astonishing revelations to women. I thought, *Really?* What were those revelations? Why were they astonishing? Finding the answers to these questions birthed a desire in me to write about what Jesus said to women. *Wonder Women of the Bible* came out in 2007, so you see *He Said What?!* was a long time in developing and wouldn't have been completed without assistance. I'm very grateful for the help of the following people.

I appreciate the staff of New Hope® Publishers for working with me on this project. I particularly appreciate Andrea Mullins's recognizing the potential of this topic; Tina Atchenson for our interesting conversations about the title and cover; Joyce Dinkins for being patient, flexible, and encouraging; and Melissa Hall and Kathryne Solomon for their editing expertise.

I thank my husband, Bob Poinsett; my friend, Jan Turner; and my sister, Judy Mills, for reading the manuscript chapter by chapter, finding errors, and giving me feedback. Their assistance was invaluable. Another friend, Janice Sitzes, gave me some feedback on a couple of the chapters as well as Carol Martino, a woman I've never met.

Pat Townsend and Linette Dunn gave me feedback during the early days of formulating the book's concept. Liz Heaney was a good sounding board during the time I was negotiating the book's contract.

I appreciate the prayers of those who prayed for me. In addition to Bob, Jan, Judy, and Janice, that would include Sue Johnson; Annette Huber; Mary Rose Fox; Carileen Bollinger; Vi Burton; and my sons, Jim, Joel, and Ben.

All of these dear people added to the richness of the writing process, and I treasure them for their interest and support. I trust the book is better because of their participation. I know I'm a better person because of their involvement in my life.